THE FATE OF THE EDSEL AND OTHER BUSINESS ADVENTURES

Books by John Brooks

THE FATE OF THE EDSEL AND OTHER BUSINESS ADVENTURES
THE SEVEN FAT YEARS
THE MAN WHO BROKE THINGS
A PRIDE OF LIONS
THE BIG WHEEL

THE FATE OF THE EDSEL AND OTHER BUSINESS ADVENTURES

by John Brooks

HARPER & ROW, PUBLISHERS
NEW YORK
AND
EVANSTON

Except for the introductory chapter, all of the material in this book appeared originally in *The New Yorker,* in somewhat different form. The author expresses his appreciation of much help and encouragement given him by the editors of *The New Yorker,* and especially by Gardner Botsford, Robert Gerdy, William Shawn, and Sanderson Vanderbilt.

FIRST EDITION

L-M

LIBRARY OF CONGRESS CATALOG CARD NUMBER: 62-20106

TO R.E.B.

Contents

Introduction: Business as Adventure

ACCORDING to Webster's *New International Dictionary* (Second Edition), one of the meanings of the word "adventure" is "a mercantile or speculative enterprise or hazard; a venture." The *Shorter Oxford English Dictionary* supplies the additional information that "adventure" has been used in this sense since 1625—or a mere fifty-five years after 1570, when it came to mean "a novel or exciting incident."

Furthermore, this dictionary authority is honored in contemporary everyday usage; for example, the various underwriting firms that join forces for the flotation of new issues of stocks or bonds are spoken of in the legal documents pertaining to their deals as "the joint adventurers." Their adventure consists of accepting the risk that the stocks or bonds can be sold to investors at a preset price within a definite period of time, and in some cases it turns out to be an adventure indeed. I suppose a female stock-and-bond underwriter is legally an adventuress, but I am not sure of this.

The point is that the language reflects the truth; business *is* an adventure, or can be. The profit motive is essential (without it, a business enterprise would be a pale sort of thing) but insufficient. To make a dollar merely so that one can spend or save it, and then go back to make another dollar, is antlike drudgery. But to make a dollar—or lose it—in a spirit of play, with a certain natural frivolity, is to measure up to human scale; to take part in a real-life game of chance; to have an adventure. In saying this I do not mean to de-emphasize the greed and rascality of some businessmen past and present, nor to ignore the vast social harm that they have done. Business, like other games, needs rules and umpires to restrain the exuberance of the competitors, and I should think—good Lord, I should hope—there will always be a few competitors who will spend their time either complaining about the rules at the top of their lungs, or else hypocritically praising the rules while secretly trying to circumvent them. Until quite recently, American business, operating in a nation founded on libertarian and laissez-faire ideas, was a game with too few rules. That situation has been largely corrected, and the rule-making apparatus has been developed to the point where new rules can in most cases be devised as needed.

All of the people in this book either approached business in an adventurous spirit or else had adventure forced upon them. Walter K. Gutman, for example, has made the classically humdrum occupation of being a security analyst into an adventure by approaching each company to be investigated as if he were a gumshoe man tracking down a picturesque wrongdoer, and each market letter to be written as if his legitimate subject were life and art as well as Lily Tulip and American Telephone. The adventure of the people of the City of London is the interesting one of trying to conduct commercial affairs with style and elegance. That of the executives in the great electrical companies who violated the Sherman Antitrust Act was of another sort. Their tangled and tragic adventure, a very modern, Kafkaesque one, seemed to be that of otherwise innocuous men blundering almost blindly into crime in a world where personal responsibility and personal identity tended to be lost in the hugeness of the organization.

These are not all success stories; a happy ending is not necessarily the criterion of a good adventure. Indeed, the opposite may be nearer the truth. In retrospect one can see that Clarence Saunders, the country boy who set out to beat Wall Street at its own game, carried within himself the seeds of his own destruction. Possibly something similar may be said about the men who built and promoted the ill-fated Edsel; after all, one of them has since said that in their enthusiasm for their creation they were "auto-intoxicated." But in both cases, the false hopes and self-delusions of the enthusiasts were their glory as well as their bane. Like the original Don Quixote, if they had had more self-knowledge and foresight, they would not have had any adventures.

THE FATE OF THE EDSEL AND OTHER BUSINESS ADVENTURES

1 / Gigantic and Full of Meaning: The Rise of the Edsel

IN THE CALENDAR of American economic life, 1955 was the Year of the Automobile. That year, American automobile makers sold over seven million passenger cars, or almost a million more than they have sold in any other year. That year, General Motors easily sold the public $325 million worth of new common stock, and the stock market as a whole, led by the motors, gyrated upward so frantically that Congress investigated it. And that year, too, the Ford Motor Company decided to produce a new automobile in what was quaintly called the medium-price range—roughly, from $2,400 to $4,000—and went ahead and designed it more or less in conformity with the fashion of the day, which was for cars that were long, wide, low, lavishly decorated with chrome, liberally supplied with gadgets, and equipped with engines of a power just barely insufficient to send them into orbit. Two years later, in September, 1957, the Ford Company put its new car, the Edsel, on the market, to the accompaniment of more fanfare than had attended the arrival of any other new car since the same company's Model A, brought out thirty years earlier. The total amount spent on the Edsel before the first specimen went on sale was announced as a quarter of a billion dollars; its launching—as *Business Week* declared and nobody cared to deny—was more costly than that of any other consumer product in history. As a starter toward getting its investment back, Ford counted on selling at least 200,000 Edsels the first year.

There may be an aborigine somewhere in a remote rain forest who hasn't yet heard that things failed to turn out that way. To be precise, two years two months and fifteen days later Ford had sold only 109,466 Edsels, and, beyond a doubt, many hundreds, if not several thousands, of those were bought by Ford executives, dealers, salesmen, advertising men, assembly-line workers, and others who had a personal interest in seeing the car succeed. The 109,466 amounted to considerably less than one percent of the passenger cars sold in the United States during that period, and on November 19, 1959, having lost, according to some outside estimates, around $350 million on the Edsel, the Ford Company permanently discontinued its production.

How could this have happened? How could a company so mightily endowed with money, experience, and, presumably, brains have been guilty of such a monumental mistake? Even before the Edsel was dropped, some of the more articulate members of the car-minded public had come forward with an answer—an answer so simple and so seemingly reasonable that, though it was not the only one advanced, it became widely accepted as the truth. The Edsel, these people argued, was designed, named, advertised, and promoted with a slavish adherence to the results of public-opinion polls and of their younger cousin, motivational research, and they concluded that when the public is wooed in an excessively calculated manner, it tends to turn away in favor of some gruffer but more spontaneously attentive suitor. A while back, in the face of an understandable reticence on the part of the Ford Motor Company, which enjoys documenting its boners no more than anyone else, I set out to learn what I could about the Edsel debacle, and my investigations have led me to believe that what we have here is less than the whole truth.

For, although the Edsel was *supposed* to be advertised, and otherwise promoted, strictly on the basis of preferences expressed in polls, some old-fashioned snake-oil-selling methods, intuitive rather than scientific, crept in. Although it was *supposed* to have been named in much the same way, science was curtly discarded at the last minute and the Edsel was named for the father of the company's president, like a nineteenth-century brand of cough drops or saddle soap. As for the design, it was arrived at without even a pretense of consulting the polls, and by the method that has been standard for years in the designing of automobiles—that of simply pooling the hunches of sundry company committees. The common explanation of the Edsel's downfall, then, under scrutiny, turns out to be largely a myth, in the colloquial sense of that term. But the facts of the case may live to become a myth of a symbolic sort—a modern American antisuccess story.

The origins of the Edsel go back to the fall of 1948, seven years before the year of decision, when Henry Ford II, who had been president and undisputed boss of the company since the death of his grandfather, the original Henry, a year earlier, proposed to the company's executive committee, which included Ernest R. Breech, the executive vice-president, that studies be undertaken concerning the wisdom of putting on the market a new and wholly different medium-priced car. The studies were undertaken. There appeared to be good reason for them. It was a well-known practice at the time for low-income owners of Fords, Plymouths, and Chevrolets to turn in their symbols of inferior caste as soon as their earnings rose above five thousand dollars a year, and "trade up" to a medium-priced car. From Ford's point of view, this would have been all well and good except that, for some reason, Ford owners usually traded up not to Mercury, the company's only medium-priced car, but to one or another of the medium-priced cars put out by its big rivals—Oldsmobile, Buick, and Pontiac, among the General Motors products, and, to a lesser extent, Dodge and De Soto, the Chrysler candidates. Lewis D. Crusoe, then a vice-president of the Ford Motor Company, was not overstating the case when he said, "We have been growing customers for General Motors."

The outbreak of the Korean War, in 1950, meant that Ford had no choice but to go on growing customers for its competitors, since introducing a new car at such a time was out of the question. The company's executive committee put aside the studies proposed by President Ford, and there matters rested for two years. Late in 1952, however, the end of the war appeared sufficiently imminent for the company to pick up where it had left off, and the studies were energetically resumed by a group called the Forward Product Planning Committee, which turned over much of the detailed work to the Lincoln-Mercury Division, under the direction of Richard Krafve (pronounced Kraffy), the division's assistant general manager. Krafve, a forceful, rather saturnine man with a habitually puzzled look, was then in his middle forties. The son of a printer on a small farm journal in Minnesota, he had been a sales engineer and management consultant before joining Ford, in 1947, and although he could not have known it in 1952, he was to have reason to look puzzled. As the man directly responsible for the Edsel and its fortunes, enjoying its brief glory and attending it in its mortal agonies, he had a rendezvous with destiny.

In December, 1954, after two years' work, the Forward Product Planning Committee submitted to the executive committee a six-volume blockbuster of a report summarizing its findings. Supported by copious statistics, the report predicted the arrival of the American millennium, or something a lot like it, in 1965. By that time, the Forward Product Planning Committee estimated, the gross national product would be $535 billion a year—up more than $135 billion in a decade. (As a matter of fact, this part of the millennium arrived much sooner than the Forward Planners estimated. The G. N. P. rate for the last quarter of 1961 was $542 billion.) The number of cars in operation would be seventy million—up twenty million. More than half the families in the nation would have incomes of over five thousand dollars a year, and more than 40 percent of all the cars sold would be in the medium-price range or better. The report's picture of America in 1965, presented in crushing detail, was of a country after Detroit's own heart—its banks oozing money, its streets and highways choked with huge, dazzling medium-priced cars, its newly rich, "upwardly mobile" citizens racked with longings for more of them. The moral was clear. If by that time Ford had not come out with a second medium-priced car—not just a new model, but a new make—and made it a favorite in its field, the company would miss out on its share of the national boodle.

On the other hand, the Ford bosses were well aware of the enormous risks connected with putting a new car on the market. They knew, for example, that of the 2,900 American makes that had been introduced since the beginning of the Automobile Age—the Black Crow (1905), the Averageman's Car (1906), the Bugmobile (1907), the Dan Patch (1911), and the Lone Star (1920) among them—only about twenty were still around. They knew all about the automotive casualties that had followed the Second World War—among them Crosley, which had given up altogether, and Kaiser Motors, which, though still alive in 1954, was breathing its last. (The members of the Forward Product Planning Committee must have glanced at each other uneasily when, a year later, Henry J. Kaiser wrote, in a valediction to his car business, "We expected to toss fifty million dollars into the automobile pond, but we didn't expect it to disappear without a ripple.") The Ford men also knew that neither of the other members of the industry's powerful and well-heeled Big Three—General Motors and Chrysler—had ventured to bring out a new standard-size make since the former's La Salle, in 1927, and the latter's Plymouth, in 1928, and that Ford itself had not attempted to turn the trick since 1938, when it launched the Mercury.

Nevertheless, the Ford men felt bullish—so remarkably bullish that they resolved to toss into the automobile pond five times the sum that Kaiser had. In April, 1955, Henry Ford II, Breech, and the other members of the executive committee officially approved the Forward Product Planning Committee's findings, and, to implement them, set up another agency, called the Special Products Division, with the star-crossed Krafve as its head. Thus the company gave its formal sanction to the efforts of its designers, who, having divined the trend of events, had already been doodling for several months on plans for a new car. Since neither they nor the newly organized Krafve outfit, when it took over, had an inkling of what the thing on their drawing boards might be called, it became known to everybody at Ford, and even in the company's press releases, as the E-Car—the "E," it was explained, standing for "Experimental."

The man directly in charge of the E-Car's design—or, to use the gruesome trade word, "styling"—was a Canadian, then not yet forty, named Roy A. Brown, who, before taking on the E-Car (and after studying industrial design at the Detroit Art Academy), had had a hand in the designing of radios, motor cruisers, colored-glass products, Cadillacs, Oldsmobiles, and Lincolns.* Brown recently recalled his aspirations as he went to work on the new project. "Our goal was to create a vehicle which would be unique in the sense that it would be readily recognizable in styling theme from the nineteen other makes of cars on the road at that time," he wrote from England, where at the time of his writing he was employed as chief stylist for the Ford Motor Company, Ltd., manufacturers of trucks, tractors, and small cars. "We went to the extent of making photographic studies from some distance of all nineteen of these cars, and it became obvious that at a distance of a few hundred feet the similarity was so great that it was practically impossible to distinguish one make from the others. . . . They were all 'peas in a pod.' We decided to select [a style that] would be 'new' in the sense that it was unique, and yet at the same time be familiar."

While the E-Car was on the drawing boards in Ford's styling studio —situated, like its administrative offices, in the company's barony of Dearborn, just outside Detroit—work on it progressed under the conditions of melodramatic, if ineffectual, secrecy that invariably attend such operations in the automobile business: locks on the studio doors that could be changed in fifteen minutes if a key should fall into enemy hands; a security force standing round-the-clock guard over the estab-

* The word "styling" is a weed deeply embedded in the garden of automobilia. In its preferred sense, the verb "to style" means to name; thus the Special Products Division's epic efforts to choose a name for the E-Car, which will be chronicled presently, were really the styling program, and what Brown and his associates were up to was something else again. In its second sense, says Webster, "to style" means "to fashion in . . . the accepted style"; this was just what Brown, who hoped to achieve originality, was trying not to do, so Brown's must have been the antistyling program. But the weed is too well rooted, its tendrils too entangling. The hell with it.

lishment; and a telescope to be trained at intervals on nearby high points of the terrain where peekers might be roosting. (All such precautions, however inspired, are doomed to fail, because none of them provide a defense against Detroit's version of the Trojan horse—the job-jumping stylist, whose cheerful treachery makes it relatively easy for the rival companies to keep tabs on what the competition is up to. No one, of course, is better aware of this than the rivals themselves, but the cloak-and-dagger stuff is thought to pay for itself in publicity value.) Twice a week or so, Krafve—head down, and sticking to low ground—made the journey to the styling studio, where he would confer with Brown, check up on the work as it proceeded, and offer advice and encouragement. Krafve was not the kind of man to envision his objective in a single revelatory flash; instead, he anatomized the styling of the E-Car into a series of laboriously minute decisions—how to shape the fenders, what pattern to use with the chrome, what kind of door handles to put on, and so on and on. If Michelangelo ever added up the number of decisions that went into the execution of, say, his "David," he kept it to himself, but Krafve, an orderly-minded man in an era of orderly-functioning computers, has calculated that in styling the E-Car he and his associates had to make up their minds on no fewer than four thousand occasions. He reasoned at the time that if they arrived at the right yes-or-no choice on every one of those occasions, they ought, in the end, to come up with a stylistically perfect car—or at least a car that would be unique and at the same time familiar. But Krafve concedes today that he found it difficult thus to bend the creative process to the yoke of system, principally because many of the four thousand decisions he made wouldn't stay put. "Once you get a general theme, you begin narrowing down," he says. "You keep modifying, and then modifying your modifications. Finally, you *have* to settle on something, because there isn't any more time. If it weren't for the deadline, you'd probably go on modifying indefinitely."

Except for later, minor modifications of the modified modifications, the E-Car had been fully styled by midsummer of 1955. As the world was to learn two years later, its most striking aspect was a novel, horse-collar-shaped radiator grille, set vertically in the center of a conventionally low, wide front end—a blend of the unique and the familiar that was there for all to see, though certainly not for all to admire. In two prominent respects, however, Brown or Krafve, or both, lost sight entirely of the familiar, specifying a unique rear end, marked by wide-spread horizontal wings that were in bold contrast to the huge longitudinal tail fins then captivating the market, and a unique cluster of automatic-transmission push buttons on the hub of the steering wheel. In a speech to the public delivered a while before the public had its first look at the car, Krafve let fall a hint or two about its styling, which, he said, made it so "distinctive" that, externally, it was "immediately recognizable from front, side, and rear," and, internally, it was "the epitome of the push-button era without wild-blue-yonder Buck Rogers concepts." At last came the day when the men in the highest stratum of the Ford hierarchy were given their first glimpse of the car. It produced an effect that was little short of apocalyptic. On August 15, 1955, in the ceremonial secrecy of the styling center, while Krafve, Brown, and their aides stood by smiling nervously and washing their hands in air, the members of the Forward Product Planning Committee, including Henry Ford II and Breech, watched critically as a curtain was lifted to reveal the first full-size model of the E-Car—a clay one, with tinfoil simulating aluminum and chrome. According to eyewitnesses, the audience sat in utter silence for what seemed like a full minute, and then, as one man, burst into a round of applause. Nothing of the kind had ever happened at an intracompany first showing at Ford since 1896, when old Henry had bolted together his first horseless carriage.

One of the most persuasive and most frequently cited explanations of the Edsel's failure is that it was a victim of the time lag between the decision to produce it and the act of putting it on the market. It is easy to see now, when smaller and less powerful cars, euphemistically called "compacts," have become so popular as to turn the old automobile status-ladder upside down, that the Edsel was a giant step in the wrong direction, but it was far from easy to see that in fat, tail-finny 1955. American ingenuity—which has produced the electric light, the flying machine, the tin Lizzie, the atomic bomb, and even a tax system that permits a man, under certain circumstances, to clear a profit by making a charitable donation—has not yet found a way of getting an automobile on the market within a reasonable time after it comes off the drawing board; the making of steel dies, the alerting of retail dealers, the preparation of advertising and promotion campaigns, the gaining of executive approval for each successive move, and the various other gavotte-like routines that are considered as vital as breathing in Detroit and its environs usually consume about two years. Guessing future tastes is hard enough for those charged with planning the customary annual changes in models of established makes; it is far harder to bring out an altogether new creation, like the E-Car, for which several intricate new steps must be worked into the dance pattern, such as endowing the product with a personality and selecting a suitable name for it, to say nothing of consulting various oracles in an effort to determine whether, by the time of the unveiling, the state of the national economy will make bringing out *any* new car seem like a good idea.

Faithfully executing the prescribed routine, the Special Products Division called upon its director of planning for market research, David Wallace, to see what he could do about imparting a personality to the E-Car and giving it a name. Wallace, a lean, craggy-jawed pipe puffer with a soft, slow, thoughtful way of speaking, gives the impression of being the Platonic idea of the college professor—the very steel die from which the breed is cut—although, in point of fact, his background is not strongly academic. Before going to Ford, in 1955, he had worked his way through Westminster College, in Pennsylvania, ridden out the depression as a construction laborer in New York City, and then spent ten years in market research at *Time*. Still, impressions are what count, and Wallace admits that during his tenure with Ford he consciously stressed his professorial air for the sake of the advantage it gave him in dealing with the bluff, practical men of Dearborn. "Our department came to be regarded as a semi-Brain Trust," he says, with a certain satisfaction. He insisted, typically, on living in Ann Arbor, where he could bask in the scholarly aura of the University of Michigan, rather than in Dearborn or Detroit, both of which he declared were intolerable after business hours. Whatever the degree of his success in projecting the image of the E-Car, he seems, by his small eccentricities, to have done splendidly at projecting the image of Wallace. "I don't think Dave's motivation for being at Ford was basically economic," his old boss, Krafve, says. "Dave is the scholarly type, and I think he considered the job an interesting challenge." One could scarcely ask for better evidence of image projection than that.

Wallace clearly recalls the reasoning—candid enough—that guided him and his assistants as they sought just the right personality for the E-Car. "We said to ourselves, 'Let's face it—there is no great difference in basic mechanism between a two-thousand-dollar Chevrolet and a six-thousand-dollar Cadillac,' " he says. " 'Forget about all the ballyhoo,' we said, 'and you'll see that they are really pretty much the same thing. Nevertheless, there's something—there's *got* to be something—in the makeup of a certain number of people that gives them a yen for a Cadillac, in spite of its high price, or maybe because of it.' We concluded that cars are the means to a sort of dream fulfillment. There's some irrational factor in people that makes them want one kind of car rather than another—something that has nothing to do with the mechanism at all but with the car's personality, as the customer imagines it. What we wanted to do, naturally, was to give the E-Car the personality that would make the greatest number of people want it. We figured we had a big advantage over the other manufacturers of medium-priced cars, because we didn't have to worry about changing a pre-existent, perhaps somewhat obnoxious personality. All we had to do was create the exact one we wanted—from scratch."

As the first step in determining what the E-Car's exact personality should be, Wallace decided to assess the personalities of the medium-priced cars already on the market, and those of the so-called low-priced cars as well, since the cost of some of the cheap cars' 1955 models had risen well up into the medium-price range. To this end, he engaged the Columbia University Bureau of Applied Social Research to interview eight hundred recent car buyers in Peoria, Illinois, and another eight hundred in San Bernardino, California, on the mental images they had of the various automobile makes concerned. (In undertaking this commercial enterprise, Columbia maintained its academic independence by reserving the right to publish its findings.) "Our idea was to get the reaction in cities, among clusters of people," Wallace says. "We didn't want a cross section. What we wanted was something that would show interpersonal factors. We picked Peoria as a place that is Midwestern, stereotyped, and not loaded with extraneous factors—like a General Motors glass plant, say. We picked San Bernardino because the West Coast is very important in the automobile business, and because the market there is quite different—people tend to buy flashier cars."

The questions that the Columbia researchers fared forth to ask in Peoria and San Bernardino dealt exhaustively with practically everything having to do with automobiles except such matters as how much they cost, how safe they were, and whether they ran. In particular, Wallace wanted to know the respondents' impressions of each of the existing makes. Who, in their opinion, would naturally own a Chevrolet or a Buick or whatever? People of what age? Of which sex? Of what social status? From the answers, Wallace found it easy to put together a personality portrait of each make. The image of the Ford came into focus as that of a very fast, strongly masculine car, of no particular social pretensions, that might characteristically be driven by a rancher or an automobile mechanic. In contrast, Chevrolet emerged as older, wiser, slower, a bit less rampantly masculine, and slightly more distingué—a clergyman's car. Buick jelled into a middle-aged lady—or, at least, more of a lady than Ford, sex in cars having proved to be relative—with a bit of the devil still in her, whose most felicitous mate would be a lawyer, a doctor, or a dance-band leader. As for the Mercury, it came out as virtually a hot rod, best suited to a young-buck racing driver; thus, despite its higher price tag, it was associated with persons having incomes no higher than the average Ford owner's, so no wonder Ford owners had not been trading up to it. This odd discrepancy between image and fact, coupled with the circumstance that, in sober truth, all four makes looked very much alike and had almost the same horsepower under their hoods, only served to bear out Wallace's premise that the automobile fancier, like a young man in love, is incapable of sizing up the object of his affections in anything resembling a rational manner.

By the time the researchers closed the books on Peoria and San Bernardino, they had elicited replies not only to these questions but to others, several of which, it would appear, only the most abstruse sociological thinker could relate to medium-priced cars. "Frankly, we dabbled," Wallace says. "It was a dragnet operation." Among the odds and ends that the dragnet dredged up were some that, when pieced together, led the researchers to report:

> By looking at those respondents whose annual incomes range from $4,000 to $11,000, we can make an . . . observation. A

> considerable percentage of these respondents [to a question about their ability to mix cocktails] are in the "somewhat" category on ability to mix cocktails. . . . Evidently, they do not have much confidence in their cocktail-mixing ability. We may infer that these respondents are aware of the fact that they are in the learning process. They may be able to mix Martinis or Manhattans, but beyond these popular drinks they don't have much of a repertoire.

Wallace, dreaming of an ideally lovable E-Car, was delighted as returns like these came pouring into his Dearborn office. But when the time for a final decision drew near, it became clear to him that he must put aside peripheral issues like cocktail-mixing prowess and address himself once more to the old problem of the image. And here, it seemed to him, the greatest pitfall was the temptation to aim, in accordance with what he took to be the trend of the times, for extremes of masculinity, youthfulness, and speed; indeed, the following passage from one of the Columbia reports, as he interpreted it, contained a specific warning against such folly:

> Offhand we might conjecture that women who drive cars probably work, and are more mobile than non-owners, and get gratifications out of mastering a traditionally male role. But . . . there is no doubt that whatever gratifications women get out of their cars, and whatever social imagery they attach to their automobiles, they do want to appear as women. Perhaps more worldly women, but women.

Early in 1956, Wallace set about summing up all of his department's findings in a report to his superiors in the Special Products Division. Entitled "The Market and Personality Objectives of the E-Car" and weighty with facts and statistics—though generously interspersed with terse sections in italics or capitals from which a hard-pressed executive could get the gist of the thing in a matter of seconds—the report first indulged in some airy, skippable philosophizing and then got down to conclusions:

> What happens when an owner sees his make as a car which a *woman* might buy, but is himself a *man?* Does this apparent inconsistency of car image and the buyer's own characteristics affect his trading plans? The answer quite definitely is *Yes.* When there is a conflict between owner characteristics and make image, there is greater planning to switch to another make. In other words, when the buyer is a different kind of person from the person he thinks would own his make, he wants to change to a make in which he, inwardly, will be more comfortable.
>
> It should be noted that "conflict," as used here, can be of two kinds. Should a make have a strong and well-defined image, it is obvious that an owner with strong opposing characteristics would be in conflict. But conflict also can occur when the make image is diffuse or weakly defined. In this case, the owner is in an equally frustrating position of not being able to get a satisfactory identification from his make.

The question, then, was how to steer between the Scylla of a too definite car personality and the Charybdis of a too weak personality. To this the report replied, "Capitalize on imagery weakness of competition," and went on to urge that in the matter of age the E-Car should take an imagery position neither too young nor too old but right alongside that of the middling Oldsmobile; that in the matter of social class, not to mince matters, "the E-Car might well take a status position just below Buick and Oldsmobile"; and that in the delicate matter of sex it should try to straddle the fence, again along with the protean Olds. In sum (and in Wallace typography):

> The most advantageous personality for the E-Car might well be THE SMART CAR FOR THE YOUNGER EXECUTIVE OR PROFESSIONAL FAMILY ON ITS WAY UP.
>
> Smart car: recognition by others of the owner's good style and taste.
>
> Younger: appealing to spirited but responsible adventurers.
>
> Executive or professional: millions pretend to this status, whether they can attain it or not.
>
> Family: not exclusively masculine; a wholesome "good" role.
>
> On Its Way Up: "The E-Car has faith in you, son; we'll help you make it!"

Before spirited but responsible adventurers could have faith in the E-Car, however, it had to have a name. Very early in its history, Krafve had suggested to members of the Ford family that the new car be named for Edsel Ford, who was the only son of old Henry; the president of the Ford Motor Company from 1918 until his death, in 1943; and the father of the new generation of Fords—Henry II, Benson, and William Clay. The three brothers had let Krafve know that their father might not have cared to have his name spinning on a million hubcaps, and they had consequently suggested that the Special Products Division start looking around for a substitute. This it did, with a zeal no less emphatic than it displayed in the personality crusade. In the late summer and early fall of 1955, Wallace hired the services of several research outfits, which sent interviewers, armed with a list of two thousand possible names, to canvass sidewalk crowds in New York, Chicago, Willow Run, and Ann Arbor. The interviewers did not ask simply what the respondent thought of some such name as Mars, Jupiter, Rover, Ariel, Arrow, Dart, or Ovation. They asked what free associations each name brought to mind, and having got an answer to this one, they asked what word or words was considered the opposite of each name, on the theory that, subliminally speaking, the opposite is as much a part of a name as the tail is of a penny. The results of all this, the Special Products Division eventually decided, were inconclusive. Meanwhile, Krafve and his men held repeated sessions in a darkened room, staring, with the aid of a spotlight, at a series of cardboard signs, each bearing a name, as, one after another, they were flipped over for their consideration. One of the men thus engaged spoke up for the name Phoenix, because of its connotations of ascendancy, and another favored Altair, on the ground that it would lead practically all alphabetical lists of cars and thus enjoy an advantage analogous to that enjoyed in the animal kingdom by the aardvark. At a certain drowsy point in one session, somebody suddenly called a halt to the card-flipping and asked, in an incredulous tone, "Didn't I see 'Buick' go by two or three cards back?" Everybody looked at Wallace, the impresario of the sessions. He puffed on his pipe, smiled an academic smile, and nodded.

The card-flipping sessions proved to be as fruitless as the sidewalk interviews, and it was at this stage of the game that Wallace, resolving to try and wring from genius what the common mind had failed to yield, entered into the celebrated car-naming correspondence with the poet Marianne Moore, which was later published in *The New Yorker* and still later, in book form, by the Morgan Library. "We should like this name . . . to convey, through association or other conjuration, some visceral feeling of elegance, fleetness, advanced features and design," Wallace wrote to Miss Moore, achieving a certain feeling of elegance himself. If it is asked who among the gods of Dearborn had the inspired and inspiriting idea of enlisting Miss Moore's services in this cause, the answer, according to Wallace, is that it was no god but the wife of one of his junior assistants—a young lady who had recently graduated from Mount Holyoke, where she had heard Miss Moore lecture. Had her husband's superiors gone a step further and actually adopted one of Miss Moore's many suggestions—Intelligent Bullet, for instance, or Utopian Turtletop, or Bullet Cloisonné, or Pastelogram, or Mongoose Civique, or Andante con Moto ("Description of a good motor?" Miss Moore queried in regard to this last)—there is no telling to what heights the E-Car might have risen, but the fact is that they didn't. Dissatisfied with both the poet's ideas and their own, the executives in the Special Products Division next called in Foote, Cone & Belding, the advertising agency that had lately been signed up to handle the E-Car account. With characteristic Madison Avenue vigor, Foote, Cone & Belding organized a competition among the employees of its New York, London, and Chicago offices, offering nothing less than one of the brand-new cars as a prize to whoever thought up an acceptable name. In no time at all, Foote, Cone & Belding had eighteen thousand names in hand, including Zoom, Zip, Benson, Henry, and Drof (if in doubt, spell it backward). Suspecting that the bosses of the Special Products Division might regard this list as a trifle unwieldy, the agency got to work and cut it down to six thousand names, which it presented to them in executive session. "There you are," a Foote, Cone man said triumphantly, flopping a sheaf of papers on the table. "Six thousand names, all alphabetized and cross-referenced."

A gasp escaped Krafve. "But we don't want six thousand names," he said. "We only want one."

The situation was critical, because the making of dies for the new car was about to begin and some of them would have to bear its name. On a Thursday, Foote, Cone & Belding canceled all leaves and instituted what is called a crash program, instructing its New York and Chicago offices to set about independently cutting down the list of six thousand names to ten and to have the job done by the end of the weekend. Before the weekend was over, the two Foote, Cone offices presented their separate lists of ten to the Special Products Division, and by an almost incredible coincidence, which all hands insist *was* a coincidence, four of the names on the two lists were the same; Corsair, Citation, Pacer, and Ranger had miraculously survived the dual scrutiny. "Corsair seemed to be head and shoulders above everything else," Wallace says. "Along with other factors in its favor, it had done splendidly in the sidewalk interviews. The free associations with Corsair were rather romantic—'pirate,' 'swashbuckler,' things like that. For its opposite, we got 'princess,' or something else attractive on that order. Just what we wanted."

Corsair or no Corsair, the E-Car was named the Edsel in the early spring of 1956, though the public was not informed until the following autumn. The epochal decision was reached at a meeting of the Ford executive committee held at a time when, as it happened, all three Ford brothers were away. In President Ford's absence, the meeting was conducted by Breech, who had become chairman of the board in 1955, and his mood that day was brusque, and not one to linger long over swashbucklers and princesses. After hearing the final choices, he said, "I don't like any of them. Let's take another look at some of the others." So they took another look at the favored rejects, among them the name Edsel, which, in spite of the three Ford brothers' expressed interpretation of their father's probable wishes, had been retained as a sort of anchor to windward. Breech led his associates in a patient scrutiny of the list until they came to "Edsel." "Let's call it that," Breech said with calm finality. There were to be four main models of the E-Car, with variations on each one, and Breech soothed some of his colleagues by adding that the magic four—Corsair, Citation, Pacer, and Ranger—might be used, if anybody felt so inclined, as the subnames for the models. A telephone call was put through to Henry II, who was vacationing in Nassau. He said that if Edsel was the choice of the executive committee, he would abide by its decision, provided he could get the approval of the rest of his family. Within a few days, he got it.

As Wallace wrote to Miss Moore a while later: "We have chosen a name. . . . It fails somewhat of the resonance, gaiety, and zest we were seeking. But it has a personal dignity and meaning to many of us here. Our name, dear Miss Moore, is—Edsel. I hope you will understand."

It may be assumed that word of the naming of the E-Car spread a certain amount of despair among the Foote, Cone & Belding backers of more metaphorical names, none of whom won a free car—a despair heightened by the fact that the name "Edsel" had been ruled out of the competition from the first. But their sense of disappointment was as nothing compared to the gloom that enveloped many employees of the Special Products Division. Some felt that the name of a former president of the company, who had sired its current president, bore dynastic connotations that were alien to the American temper; others, who, with Wallace, had put their trust in the quirks of the mass unconscious, believed that "Edsel" was a disastrously unfortunate combination of syllables. What were its free associations? Pretzel, diesel, hard sell. What was its opposite? It didn't seem to have any. Still, the matter was settled, and there was nothing to do but put the best possible face on it. Besides, the anguish in the Special Products Division was by no means unanimous, and Krafve himself, of course, was among those who had no objection to the name. He still has none, declining to go along with those who contend that the decline and fall of the Edsel may be dated from the moment of its christening.

Krafve, in fact, was so well pleased with the way matters had turned out that when, at eleven o'clock on the morning of November 19, 1956, after a long summer of thoughtful silence, the Ford Company released to the world the glad tidings that the E-Car had been named the Edsel, he accompanied the announcement with a few dramatic flourishes of his own. On the very stroke of that hour on that day, the telephone operators in Krafve's domain began greeting callers with "Edsel Division" instead of "Special Products Division"; all stationery bearing the obsolete letterhead of the division vanished and was replaced by sheaves of paper headed "Edsel Division"; and outside the building a huge stainless-steel sign reading "EDSEL DIVISION" rose ceremoniously to the rooftop. Krafve himself managed to remain earthbound, though he had his own reasons for feeling buoyant; in recognition of his leadership of the E-Car project up to that point, he was given the august title of Vice-President of the Ford Motor Company and General Manager, Edsel Division.

From the administrative point of view, this off-with-the-old-on-with-the-new effect was merely harmless window dressing. In the strict secrecy of the Dearborn test track, vibrant, almost full-fledged Edsels, with their name graven on their superstructures, were already being road-tested; Brown and his fellow stylists were already well along with their designs for the *next* year's Edsel; recruits were already being signed up for an entirely new organization of retail dealers to sell the Edsel to the public; and Foote, Cone & Belding, having been relieved of the burden of staging crash programs to collect names and crash programs to get rid of them again, was already deep in schemes for advertising the Edsel, under the personal direction of a no less substantial pillar of his trade than Fairfax M. Cone, the agency's head man. In planning his campaign, Cone relied heavily on what had come to be called the "Wallace prescription"; that is, the formula for the Edsel's personality as set forth by Wallace back in the days before the big naming bee—"The smart car for the younger executive or professional family on its way up." So enthusiastic was Cone about the prescription that he accepted it with only one revision—the substitution of "middle-income" family for "younger executive," his hunch being that there were more middle-income families around than young executives, or even people who *thought* they were young executives. In an expansive mood, possibly induced by his having landed an account that was expected to bring billings of well over ten million dollars a year, Cone described to reporters on several occasions the kind of campaign he was plotting for the Edsel—quiet, self-assured, and avoiding as much as possible the use of the adjective "new," which, though it had an obvious application to the product, he considered rather lacking in cachet. Above all, the campaign was to be classic in its calmness. "We think it would be awful for the advertising to compete with the car," Cone told the press. "We hope that no one will ever ask, 'Say, did you see that Edsel ad?' in any newspaper or magazine or on television, but, instead, that hundreds of thousands of people will say, and say again, 'Man, did you read about that Edsel?' or 'Did you see that car?' This is the difference between advertising and selling." Evidently enough, Cone felt confident about the campaign and the Edsel. Like a chess master who has no doubt that he will win, he could afford to explicate the brilliance of his moves even as he made them.

Automobile men still talk, with admiration for the virtuosity displayed and a shudder at the ultimate outcome, of the Edsel Division's drive to round up retail dealers. Ordinarily, an established manufacturer launches a new car through dealers who are already handling his other makes and who, to begin with, take on the upstart as a sort of sideline. Not so in the case of the Edsel; Krafve received authorization from on high to go all out and build up a retail-dealer organization by making raids on dealers who had contracts with other manufacturers, or even with the other Ford Company divisions—Ford and Lincoln-Mercury. (Although the Ford dealers thus corralled were not obliged to cancel their old contracts, all the emphasis was on signing up retail outlets exclusively dedicated to the selling of Edsels.) The goal set for Introduction Day—which, after a great deal of soul-searching, was finally established as September 4, 1957—was twelve hundred Edsel dealers from coast to coast. They were not to be just any dealers, either; Krafve made it clear that Edsel was interested in signing up only dealers whose records showed that they had a marked ability to sell cars without resorting to the high-pressure tricks of borderline legality that had lately been giving the automobile business a bad name. "We simply have to have quality dealers with quality service facilities," Krafve said. "A customer who gets poor service on an established brand blames the dealer. On an Edsel, he will blame the car." The goal of twelve hundred was a high one, for no dealer, quality or not, can afford to switch makes lightly. The average dealer has at least a hundred thousand dollars tied up in his agency, and in large cities the investment is much higher. He must hire salesmen, mechanics, and office help; buy his own tools, technical literature, and signs, the latter costing as much as five thousand dollars a set; and pay the factory spot cash for the cars he receives from it.

The man charged with mobilizing an Edsel sales force along these exacting lines was J. C. (Larry) Doyle, who, as general sales-and-marketing manager of the division, ranked second to Krafve himself. A veteran of forty years with the Ford Company, who had started with it as an office boy in Kansas City and had spent the intervening time mainly selling, Doyle was a maverick in his field. On the one hand, he had an air of kindness and consideration that made him the very antithesis of the glib, brash denizens of a thousand automobile rows across the continent, and, on the other, he did not trouble to conceal an old-time salesman's skepticism about such things as analyzing the sex and status of automobiles, a pursuit he characterized by saying, "When I play pool, I like to keep one foot on the floor." Still, he knew how to sell cars, and that was what the Edsel Division needed. Recalling how he and his sales staff brought off the unlikely trick of persuading substantial and reputable men who had already achieved success in one of the toughest of all businesses to tear up profitable franchises in favor of a risky new one, Doyle said not long ago, "As soon as the first few new Edsels came through, early in 1957, we put a couple of them in each of our five regional sales offices. Needless to say, we kept those offices locked and the blinds drawn. Dealers in every make for miles around wanted to see the car, if only out of curiosity, and that gave us the leverage we needed. We let it be known that we would show the car only to dealers who were really interested in coming with us, and then we sent our regional field managers out to surrounding towns to try to line up the No. 1 dealer in each to see the cars. If we couldn't get No. 1, we'd try for No. 2. Anyway, we set things up so that no one got in to see the Edsel without listening to a complete one-hour pitch on the whole situation by a member of our sales force. It worked very well." It worked so well that by midsummer, 1957, it was clear that Edsel was going to have a lot of quality dealers on Introduction Day. (In fact, it missed the goal of twelve hundred by a couple of dozen.) Indeed, some dealers in other makes were apparently so confident of the Edsel's success, or so bemused by the Doyle staff's pitch, that they were entirely willing to sign up after hardly more than a glance at the Edsel itself. Doyle's people urged them to study the car closely, and kept reciting the litany of its virtues, but the prospective Edsel dealers would wave such protestations aside and demand a contract without further ado. In retrospect, it would seem that Doyle could have given lessons to the Pied Piper.

Now that the Edsel was no longer the exclusive concern of Dearborn, the Ford Company was irrevocably committed to going ahead. "Until Doyle went into action, the whole program could have been quietly dropped at any time at a word from top management, but once the dealers had been signed up, there was the matter of honoring your contract to put out a car," Krafve has explained. The matter was attended to with dispatch. Early in June, 1957, the company announced that of the $250 million it had set aside to defray the advance costs of the Edsel, $150 million was being spent on basic facilities, including the conversion of various Ford and Mercury plants to the needs of producing the new cars; $50 million on special Edsel tooling; and $50 million on initial advertising and promotion. In June, too, an Edsel destined to be the star of a television commercial for future release was stealthily transported in a closed van to Hollywood, where, on a locked sound stage patrolled by security guards, it was exposed to the cameras in the admiring presence of a few carefully chosen actors who had sworn that their lips would be sealed from then until Introduction Day. For this delicate photographic operation the Edsel Division cannily enlisted the services of Cascade Pictures, which also worked for the Atomic Energy Commission, and, as far as is known, there were no unintentional leaks. "We took all the same precautions we take for our A.E.C. films," a grim Cascade official has since said.

Within a few weeks, the Edsel Division had eighteen hundred salaried employees and was rapidly filling some fifteen thousand factory jobs in the newly converted plants. On July 15th, Edsels began rolling off assembly lines at Somerville, Massachusetts; Mahwah, New Jersey; Louisville, Kentucky; and San Jose, California. The same day, Doyle scored an important coup by signing up Charles Kreisler, a Manhattan dealer regarded as one of the country's foremost practitioners in his field, who had represented Oldsmobile—one of Edsel's self-designated rivals—before heeding the siren song from Dearborn. On July 22nd, the first advertisement for the Edsel appeared—in *Life*. A two-page spread in plain black-and-white, it was impeccably classic and calm, showing a car whooshing down a country highway at such high speed that it was an indistinguishable blur. "Lately, some mysterious automobiles have been seen on the roads," the accompanying text was headed. It went on to say that the blur was an Edsel being road-tested, and concluded with the assurance "The Edsel is on its way." Two weeks later, a second ad appeared in *Life,* this one showing a ghostly-looking car, covered with a white sheet, standing at the entrance to the Ford styling center. This time the headline read, "A man in your town recently made a decision that will change his life." The decision, it was explained, was to become an Edsel dealer. Whoever wrote the ad cannot have known how truly he spoke.

During the tense summer of 1957, the man of the hour at Edsel was C. Gayle Warnock, director of public relations, whose duty was not so much to generate public interest in the forthcoming product, there being an abundance of that, as to keep the interest at white heat, and readily convertible into a desire to buy one of the new cars on or after Introduction Day—or, as the company came to call it, Edsel Day. Warnock, a dapper, affable man with a tiny mustache, is a native of Converse, Indiana, who, long before Krafve drafted him from the Ford office in Chicago, did a spot of publicity work for county fairs—a background that has enabled him to spice the honeyed smoothness of the modern public-relations man with a touch of the old carnival pitchman's uninhibited spirit. Recalling his summons to Dearborn, Warnock says, "When Dick Krafve hired me, back in the fall of 1955, he told me, 'I want you to program the E-Car publicity from now to Introduction Day.' I said, 'Frankly, Dick, what do you mean by "program"?' He said he meant to sort of space it out, starting at the end and working backward. This was something new to me—I was used to taking what breaks I could get when I could get them—but I soon found out how right Dick was. It was almost too easy to get publicity for the Edsel. Early in 1956, when it was still called the E-Car, Krafve gave a little talk about it out in Portland, Oregon. We didn't try for anything more than a play in the local press, but the wire services picked the story up and it went out all over the country. Clippings came in by the bushel. Right then I realized the trouble we might be headed for. The public was getting to be hysterical to see our car, figuring it was going to be some kind of dream car—like nothing they'd ever seen. I said to Krafve, 'When they find out it's got four wheels and one engine, just like the next car, they're liable to be disappointed.' "

It was agreed that the safest way to tread the tightrope between overplaying and underplaying the Edsel would be to say nothing about the car as a whole but to reveal its individual charms a little at a time—a sort of automotive strip tease (a phrase that Warnock couldn't with proper dignity use himself but was happy to see the *New York Times* use for him). The policy was later violated now and then, purposely or inadvertently. For one thing, as the pre-Edsel Day summer wore on, reporters prevailed upon Krafve to authorize Warnock to show the Edsel to them, one at a time, on what Warnock called a "peeka-boo," or "you've-seen-it-now-forget-it," basis. And, for another, Edsels loaded on vans for delivery to dealers were appearing on the highways in ever-increasing numbers, covered fore and aft with canvas flaps that, as if to whet the desire of the motoring public, were forever blowing loose. That summer, too, was a time of speechmaking by an Edsel foursome consisting of Krafve, Doyle, J. Emmet Judge, who was Edsel's director of merchandise and product planning, and Robert F. G. Copeland, its assistant general sales manager for advertising, sales promotion, and training. Ranging separately up and down and across the nation, the four orators moved around so fast and so tirelessly that Warnock, lest he lose track of them, took to indicating their whereabouts with colored pins on a map in his office. "Let's see, Krafve goes from Atlanta to New Orleans, Doyle from Council Bluffs to Salt Lake City," Warnock would muse of a morning in Dearborn, sipping his second cup of coffee and then getting up to yank the pins out and jab them in again.

Although most of Krafve's audiences consisted of bankers and representatives of finance companies who it was hoped would lend money to Edsel dealers, his speeches that summer, far from echoing the general hoopla, were almost statesmanlike in their cautious—even somber—references to the new car's prospects. And well they might have been, for developments in the general economic outlook of the nation were making more sanguine men than Krafve look puzzled. In July, 1957, the stock market went into a nose dive, marking the beginning of what is now recalled as the recession of 1958. Then, early in August, a decline in the sales of medium-priced 1957 cars of all makes set in, and the general situation worsened so rapidly that, before the month was out, *Automotive News* reported that dealers in all makes were ending their season with the second-largest number of unsold new cars in history. If Krafve, on his lonely rounds, ever considered retreating to Dearborn for consolation, he was forced to put that notion out of his mind when, also in August, Mercury, Edsel's own stablemate, served notice that it was going to make things as tough as possible for the newcomer by undertaking a million-dollar, thirty-day advertising drive aimed especially at "price-conscious buyers"—a clear reference to the fact that the 1957 Mercury, which was then being sold at a discount by most dealers, cost less than the new Edsel was expected to. Meanwhile, sales of the Rambler, which was the only American-made small car then in production, were beginning to rise ominously. In the face of all these evil portents, Krafve fell into the habit of ending his speeches with a rather downbeat anecdote about the board chairman of an unsuccessful dog-food company who said to his fellow directors, "Gentlemen, let's face facts—dogs don't like our product." "As far as we're concerned," Krafve added on at least one occasion, driving home the moral with admirable clarity, "a lot will depend on whether people like our car or not."

But most of the other Edsel men were unimpressed by Krafve's misgivings. Perhaps the least impressed of all was Judge, who, while doing his bit as an itinerant speaker, specialized in community and civic groups. Undismayed by the limitations of the strip-tease policy, Judge brightened up his lectures by showing such a bewildering array of animated graphs, cartoons, charts, and pictures of parts of the car —all flashed on a CinemaScope screen—that his listeners usually got halfway home before they realized that he hadn't shown them an Edsel. He wandered restlessly around the auditorium as he spoke, shifting the kaleidoscopic images on the screen at will with the aid of an automatic slide changer—a trick made possible by a crew of electricians who laced the place in advance with a maze of wires linking the device to dozens of floor switches, which, scattered about the hall, responded when he kicked them. Each of the "Judge spectaculars," as these performances came to be known, cost the Edsel Division five thousand dollars—a sum that included the pay and expenses of the technical crew, who would arrive on the scene a day or so ahead of time to set up the electrical rig. At the last moment, Judge would descend melodramatically on the town by plane, hasten to the hall, and go into his act. "One of the greatest aspects of this whole Edsel program is the philosophy of product and merchandising behind it," Judge might start off, with a desultory kick at a switch here, a switch there. "All of us who have been a part of it are real proud of this background and we are anxiously awaiting its success when the car is introduced this fall. . . . Never again will we be associated with anything as gigantic and full of meaning as this particular program. . . . Here is a glimpse of the car which will be before the American public on September 4, 1957 [at this point, Judge would show a provocative slide of a hubcap or section of fender]. . . . It is a different car in every respect, yet it has an element of conservatism which will give it maximum appeal. . . . The distinctiveness of the frontal styling integrates with the sculptured patterns of the side treatment. . . ." And on and on Judge would rhapsodize, rolling out such awesome phrases as "sculptured sheet metal," "highlight character," and "graceful, flowing lines." At last would come the ringing peroration. "We are proud of the Edsel!" he would cry, kicking switches right and left. "When it is introduced this fall, it will take its place on the streets and highways of America, bringing new greatness to the Ford Motor Company. This is the Edsel story."

The drum-roll climax of the strip tease was a three-day press preview of the Edsel, undraped from pinched-in snout to flaring rear, that was held in Detroit and Dearborn on August 26th, 27th, and 28th, with 250 reporters from all over the country in attendance. It differed from previous automotive jamborees of its kind in that the journalists were invited to bring their wives along—and many of them did. Before it was over, it had cost the Ford Company ninety thousand dollars. Grand as it was, the conventionality of its setting was a disappointment to Warnock, who had proposed, and seen rejected, three locales that he thought would provide a more offbeat *ambiance*—a steamer on the Detroit River ("wrong symbolism"); Edsel, Kentucky ("inaccessible by road"); and Haiti ("just turned down flat"). Thus hobbled, Warnock could do no better for the reporters and their wives when they converged on the Detroit scene on Sunday evening, August 25th, than to put them up at the discouragingly named Sheraton-Cadillac Hotel and to arrange for them to spend Monday afternoon hearing and reading about the long-awaited details of the entire crop of Edsels—eighteen varieties available, in four main lines (Corsair, Citation, Pacer, and Ranger), differing mainly in their size, power, and trim. The next morning, specimens of the models themselves were revealed to the reporters in the styling center's rotunda, and Henry II offered a few words of tribute to his father. "The wives were not asked to the unveiling," a Foote, Cone man who helped plan the affair recalls. "It was too solemn and businesslike an event for that. It went over fine. There was excitement even among the hardened newspapermen." (The import of the stories that most of the excited newspapermen filed was that the Edsel seemed to be a good car, though not so radical as its billing had suggested.)

In the afternoon, the reporters were whisked out to the test track to see a team of stunt drivers put the Edsel through its paces. This event, calculated to be thrilling, turned out to be hair-raising, and even, for some, a little unstringing. Enjoined not to talk too much about speed and horsepower, since only a few months previously the whole automobile industry had nobly resolved to concentrate on making cars instead of delayed-action bombs, Warnock had decided to emphasize the Edsel's liveliness through deeds rather than words, and to accomplish this he had hired a team of stunt drivers. Edsels ran over two-foot ramps on two wheels, bounced from higher ramps on all four wheels, were driven in crisscross patterns, grazing each other, at sixty or seventy miles per hour, and skidded into complete turns at fifty. For comic relief, there was a clown driver parodying the daredevil stuff. All the while, the voice of Neil L. Blume, Edsel's engineering chief, could be heard on a loudspeaker, purring about "the capabilities, the safety, the ruggedness, the maneuverability and performance of these new cars," and skirting the words "speed" and "horsepower" as delicately as a sandpiper skirts a wave. At one point, when an Edsel leaping a high ramp just missed turning over, Krafve's face took on a ghastly pallor; he later reported that he had not known the daredevil stunts were going to be so extreme, and was concerned both for the good name of the Edsel and the lives of the drivers. Warnock, noticing his boss's distress, went over and asked Krafve if he was enjoying the show. Krafve replied tersely that he would answer when it was over and all hands safe. But everyone else seemed to be having a grand time. The Foote, Cone man said, "You looked over this green Michigan hill, and there were those glorious Edsels, performing gloriously in unison. It was beautiful. It was like the Rockettes. It was exciting. Morale was high."

Warnock's high spirits had carried him to even wilder extremes of fancy. The stunt driving, like the unveiling, was considered too rich for the blood of the wives, but the resourceful Warnock was ready for them with a fashion show that he hoped they would find at least equally diverting. He need not have worried. The star of the show, who was introduced by Brown, the Edsel stylist, as a Paris *couturière,* both beautiful and talented, turned out at the final curtain to be a female impersonator—a fact of which Warnock, to heighten the verisimilitude of the act, had given Brown no advance warning. Things have not been quite the same since between Brown and Warnock, but the wives were able to give their husbands an extra paragraph or two for their stories.

That evening, there was a big gala for one and all at the styling center, which was itself styled as a night club for the occasion, complete with a fountain that danced in time with the music of Ray McKinley's band, whose emblem, the letters "GM"—a holdover from the days of its founder, the late Glenn Miller—was emblazoned, as usual, on the music stand of each musician, very nearly ruining the evening for Warnock. The next morning, at a windup press conference held by Ford officials, Breech declared of the Edsel, "It's a husky youngster, and, like most other new parents, we're proud enough to pop our buttons." Then seventy-one of the reporters took the wheels of as many Edsels and set out for home—not to drive the cars into their garages but to deliver them to the showrooms of their local Edsel dealers. Let Warnock describe the highlights of this final flourish: "There were several unfortunate occurrences. One guy simply miscalculated and cracked up his car running into something. No fault of the Edsel *there.* One car lost its oil pan, so naturally the motor froze. It can happen to the best of cars. Fortunately, at the time of this malfunction the driver was going through a beautiful-sounding town—Paradise, Kansas, I think it was—and that gave the news reports about it a nice little positive touch. The nearest dealer gave the reporter a new Edsel, and he drove on home, climbing Pikes Peak on the way. Then one car crashed through a tollgate when the brakes failed. That was bad. It's funny, but the thing we were most worried about—other drivers being so eager to get a look at the Edsels that they'd crowd our cars off the road—happened only once. That was on the Pennsylvania Turnpike. One of our reporters was tooling along—no problems—when a Plymouth driver pulled up alongside to rubberneck, and edged so close that the Edsel got sideswiped. Minor damage."

Late in 1959, immediately after the demise of the Edsel, *Business Week* stated that at the big press preview a Ford executive had said to a reporter, "If the company weren't in so deep, we never would have brought it out now." However, since *Business Week* neglected to publish this patently sensational statement for over two years, and since to this day all the former ranking Edsel executives (Krafve included, notwithstanding his preoccupation with the luckless dog-food company) firmly maintained that right up to Edsel Day and even for a short time thereafter they expected the Edsel to succeed, it would seem that the quotation should be regarded as a highly suspect archaeological find. Indeed, during the period between the press preview and Edsel Day the spirit of everybody associated with the venture seems to have been one of wild optimism. "Oldsmobile, Goodbye!" ran the headline on an ad, in the Detroit *Free Press,* for an agency that was switching from Olds to Edsel. A dealer in Portland, Oregon, reported that he had already sold two Edsels, sight unseen. Warnock dug up a fireworks company in Japan willing to make him, at nine dollars apiece, five thousand rockets that, exploding in mid-air, would release nine-foot scale-model Edsels made of rice paper that would inflate and descend like parachutes; his head reeling with visions of filling America's skies as well as its highways with Edsels on Edsel Day, Warnock was about to dash off an order when Krafve, looking something more than puzzled, shook his head.

On September 3rd—E Day-minus-one—the prices of the various Edsel models were announced; for cars delivered to New York they ran from just under $2,800 to just over $4,100. On E Day, the Edsel arrived. In Cambridge, a band led a gleaming motorcade of the new cars up Massachusetts Avenue; flying out of Richmond, California, a helicopter hired by one of the most jubilant of the dealers lassoed by Doyle spread a giant Edsel sign above San Francisco Bay; and all over the nation, from the Louisiana bayous to the peak of Mount Rainier to the Maine woods, one needed only a radio or a television set to know that the very air, despite Warnock's setback on the rockets, was quivering with the presence of the Edsel. The tone for Edsel Day's blizzard of publicity was set by an ad, published in newspapers all over the country, in which the Edsel shared the spotlight with the Ford Company's President Ford and Chairman Breech. In the ad, Ford looked like a dignified young father, Breech like a dignified gentleman holding a full house against a possible straight, the Edsel just looked like an Edsel. The accompanying text declared that the decision to produce the car had been "based on what we knew, guessed, felt, believed, suspected—about you," and added, "YOU are the reason behind the Edsel." The tone was calm and confident. There did not seem to be much room for doubt about the reality of that full house.

Before sundown, it was estimated, 2,850,000 people had seen the new car in dealers' showrooms. Three days later, in North Philadelphia, an Edsel was stolen. It can reasonably be argued that the crime marked the high-water mark of public acceptance of the Edsel; only a few months later, any but the least fastidious of car thieves might not have bothered.

2 / Epitome: The Fall of the Edsel

THE MOST STRIKING physical characteristic of the Edsel was, of course, its radiator grille. This, in contrast to the wide and horizontal grilles of all nineteen other American makes of the time, was slender and vertical. Of chromium-plated steel, and shaped something like an egg, it sat in the middle of the car's front end, and was embellished by the word "EDSEL" in aluminum letters running down its length. It was intended to suggest the front end of practically any car of twenty or thirty years ago and of most contemporary European cars, and thus to look at once seasoned and sophisticated. The trouble was that whereas the front ends of the antiques and the European cars were themselves high and narrow—consisting, indeed, of little more than the radiator grilles—the front end of the Edsel was broad and low, just like the front ends of all its American competitors. Consequently, there were wide areas on either side of the grille that had to be filled in with something, and filled in they were—with twin panels of entirely conventional horizontal chrome grillwork. The effect was that of an Oldsmobile with the prow of a Pierce-Arrow implanted in its front end, or, more metaphorically, of the charwoman trying on the duchess' necklace. The attempt at sophistication was so transparent as to be endearing.

But if the grille of the Edsel appealed through guilelessness, the rear end was another matter. Here, too, there was a marked departure from the conventional design of the day. Instead of the notorious tail fin, the car had what looked to its fanciers like wings and to others, less ethereal-minded, like eyebrows. The lines of the trunk lid and the rear fenders, swooping upward and outward, did somewhat resemble the wings of a gull in flight, but the resemblance was marred by two long, narrow tail lights, set partly in the trunk lid and partly in the fenders, which followed those lines and created the startling illusion, especially at night, of a slant-eyed grin. From the front, the Edsel seemed, above all, anxious to please, even at the cost of being clownish; from the rear it looked crafty, Oriental, smug, one-up—maybe a little cynical and contemptuous, too. It was as if, somewhere between grille and rear fenders, a sinister personality change had taken place.

In other respects, the exterior styling of the Edsel was not far out of the ordinary. Its sides were festooned with a bit less than the average amount of chrome, and distinguished by a gouged-out bullet-shaped groove extending forward from the rear fender for about half the length of the car. Midway along this groove, the word "EDSEL" was displayed in chrome letters, and just below the rear window was a small grille-like decoration, on which was spelled out—of all things—"EDSEL." (After all, hadn't Stylist Brown declared his intention to create a vehicle that would be "readily recognizable"?) In its interior, the Edsel strove mightily to live up to the prediction of General Manager Krafve that the car would be "the epitome of the push-button era." The push-button era in medium-priced cars being what it was, Krafve's had been a rash prophecy indeed, but the Edsel rose to it with a devilish assemblage of gadgets such as had seldom, if ever, been seen before. On or near the Edsel's dashboard were a push button that popped the trunk lid open; a lever that popped the hood open; a lever that released the parking brake; a speedometer that glowed red when the driver exceeded his chosen maximum speed; a single-dial control for both heating and cooling; a tachometer, in the best racing-car style; buttons to operate or regulate the lights, the height of the radio antenna, the heater-blower, the windshield wiper, and the cigarette lighter; and a row of eight red lights to wink warnings that the engine was too hot, that it wasn't hot enough, that the generator was on the blink, that the parking brake was on, that a door was open, that the oil pressure was low, that the oil level was low, and that the gasoline level was low, the last of which the skeptical driver could confirm by consulting the gas gauge, mounted a few inches away. Epitomizing this epitome, the automatic-transmission control box—arrestingly situated on top of the steering post, in the center of the wheel—sprouted a galaxy of five push buttons so light to the touch that, as Edsel men could hardly be restrained from demonstrating, they could be depressed with a toothpick.

Of the four lines of Edsels, both of the two larger and more expensive ones—the Corsair and the Citation—were 219 inches long, or two inches longer than the biggest of the Oldsmobiles; both were eighty inches wide, or about as wide as passenger cars ever get; and the height of both was only fifty-seven inches, as low as any other medium-priced car. The Ranger and the Pacer, the smaller Edsels, were six inches shorter, an inch narrower, and an inch lower than the Corsair and the Citation. The Corsair and the Citation were equipped with 345-horsepower engines, making them more powerful than any other American car at the time of their debut, and the Ranger and the Pacer were good for 303 horsepower, near the top in their class. At the touch of a toothpick to the "Drive" button, an idling Corsair or Citation sedan (more than two tons of car, in either case) could, if properly skippered, take off with such abruptness that in ten and three-tenths seconds it would be doing a mile a minute, and in seventeen and a half seconds it would be a quarter of a mile down the road. If anything or anybody happened to be in the way when the toothpick touched the push button, so much the worse.

When the wraps were taken off the Edsel, it received what is known in the theatrical business as a mixed press. The automotive editors of the daily newspapers stuck mostly to straight descriptions of the car, with only here and there a phrase or two of appraisal, some of it ambiguous ("The difference in style is spectacular," noted Joseph C. Ingraham in the *New York Times*) and some of it openly favorable ("A handsome and hard-punching newcomer," said Fred Olmstead, in the Detroit *Free Press*). Magazine criticism was generally more exhaustive and occasionally more severe. *Motor Trend,* the largest monthly devoted to ordinary automobiles, as distinct from hot rods, devoted eight pages of its October, 1957, issue to an analysis and critique of the Edsel by Joe H. Wherry, its Detroit editor. Wherry liked the car's appearance, its interior comfort, and its gadgets, although he did not always make it clear just why; in paying his respects to the transmission buttons on the steering post, he wrote, "You need not take your eyes off the road for an instant." He conceded that there were "untold opportunities for more . . . unique approaches," but he summed up his opinion in a sentence that fairly peppered the Edsel with honorific adverbs: "The Edsel performs fine, rides well, and handles good." Tom McCahill, of *Mechanix Illustrated,* generally admired the "bolt bag," as he affectionately called the Edsel, but he had some reservations, which, incidentally, throw some interesting light on an automobile critic's equivalent of an aisle seat. "On ribbed concrete," he reported, "every time I shot the throttle to the floor quickly, the wheels spun like a gone-wild Waring Blendor. . . . At high speeds, especially through rough corners, I found the suspension a little too horsebacky. . . . I couldn't help but wonder what this salami would really do if it had enough road adhesion."

By far the most downright—and very likely the most damaging—panning that the Edsel got during its first months appeared in the January, 1958, issue of the Consumers Union monthly, *Consumer Reports,* whose 800,000 subscribers probably included more potential Edsel buyers than have ever turned the pages of *Motor Trend* or *Mechanix Illustrated.* After having put a Corsair through a series of road tests, *Consumer Reports* declared:

> The Edsel has no important basic advantages over other brands. The car is almost entirely conventional in construction. . . . The amount of shake present in this Corsair body on rough roads—which wasn't long in making itself heard as squeaks and rattles—went well beyond any acceptable limit. . . . The Corsair's handling qualities—sluggish, over-slow steering, sway and lean on turns, and a general detached-from-the-road feel—are, to put it mildly, without distinction. As a matter of simple fact, combined with the car's tendency to shake like jelly, Edsel handling represents retrogression rather than progress. . . . Stepping on the gas in traffic, or in passing cars, or just to feel the pleasurable surge of power, will cause those big cylinders really to lap up fuel. . . . The center of the steering wheel is not, in CU's opinion, a good pushbutton location. . . . To look at the Edsel

buttons pulls the driver's eyes clear down off the road. [*Pace* Mr. Wherry.] The "luxury-loaded" Edsel—as one magazine cover described it—will certainly please anyone who confuses gadgetry with true luxury.

Three months later, in a roundup of all the 1958-model cars, *Consumer Reports* went at the Edsel again, calling it "more uselessly overpowered . . . more gadget bedecked, more hung with expensive accessories than any car in its price class," and giving the Corsair and the Citation the bottom position in its competitive ratings. Like Krafve, *Consumer Reports* considered the Edsel an epitome; unlike Krafve, the magazine concluded that the car seemed to "epitomize the many excesses" with which Detroit manufacturers were "repulsing more and more potential car buyers."

And yet, in a way, the Edsel wasn't so bad. It embodied much of the spirit of its time—or at least of the time when it was designed, early in 1955. It was clumsy, powerful, dowdy, gauche, well-meaning —a de Kooning woman. Few people, apart from employees of Foote, Cone & Belding, who were paid to do so, have adequately hymned its ability, at its best, to coax and jolly the harried owner into a sense of well-being. Furthermore, the designers of several rival makes, including Chevrolet, Buick, and Ford, Edsel's own stablemate, later flattered Brown's styling by imitating at least one feature of the car's much reviled lines—the rear-end wing theme. The Edsel was obviously jinxed, but to say that it was jinxed by its design alone would be an oversimplification, as it would be to say that it was jinxed by an excess of motivational research. The fact is that in the short, unhappy life of the Edsel a number of other factors contributed to its commercial downfall. One of these was the scarcely believable circumstance that many of the very first Edsels—those obviously destined for the most glaring public limelight—were dramatically imperfect. By its preliminary program of promotion and advertising, the Ford Company had built up an overwhelming head of public interest in the Edsel, causing its arrival to be anticipated and the car itself to be gawked at with more eagerness than had ever greeted any automobile before it. After all that, it seemed, the car didn't quite work. Within a few weeks after the Edsel was introduced, its pratfalls were the talk of the land. Edsels were delivered with oil leaks, sticking hoods, trunks that wouldn't open, and push buttons that, far from yielding to a toothpick, couldn't be budged with a hammer. *Automotive News* reported that in general the earliest Edsels suffered from poor paint, inferior sheet metal, and faulty accessories, and quoted the lament of a dealer about one of the first Edsel convertibles he received: "The top was badly set, doors cockeyed, the header bar trimmed at the wrong angle, and the front springs sagged." The Ford Company had the particular bad luck to sell to Consumers Union—which buys its test cars in the open market, as a precaution against being favored with specially doctored samples—an Edsel in which the axle ratio was wrong, an expansion plug in the cooling system blew out, the power-steering pump leaked, the rear-axle gears were noisy, and the heater emitted blasts of hot air when it was turned off. A former executive of the Edsel Division has estimated that only about half of the first Edsels really performed properly.

A layman cannot help wondering how the Ford Company, in all its power and glory, could have been guilty of such a Mack Sennett routine of buildup and anticlimax. The wan, hard-working Krafve explains gamely that when a company brings out a new model of any make—even an old and tested one—the first cars often have bugs in them. A more startling theory—though only a theory—is that there may have been sabotage in some of the four plants that assembled the Edsel, all but one of which had previously been, and currently also were, assembling Fords or Mercurys. In marketing the Edsel, the Ford Company took a leaf out of the book of General Motors, which for years had successfully been permitting, and even encouraging, the makers and sellers of its Oldsmobiles, Buicks, Pontiacs, and the higher-priced models of its Chevrolet to fight for customers with no quarter given; faced with the same sort of intramural competition, some members of the Ford and Lincoln-Mercury Divisions of the Ford Company openly hoped from the start for the Edsel's downfall. (Krafve, realizing what might happen, had asked that the Edsel be assembled in plants of its own, but his superiors turned him down.) However, Doyle, speaking with the authority of a veteran of the automobile business as well as with that of Krafve's second-in-command, pooh-poohs the notion that the Edsel was the victim of dirty work at the plants. "Of course the Ford and Lincoln-Mercury Divisions didn't want to see another Ford Company car in the field," he says, "but as far as I know, anything they did at the executive and plant levels was in competitive good taste. On the other hand, at the distribution and dealer level, you got some rough infighting in terms of whispering and propaganda. If I'd been in one of the other divisions, I'd have done the same thing." No proud defeated general of the old school ever spoke more nobly.

It is a tribute of sorts to the men who gave the Edsel its big buildup that although cars tending to rattle, balk, and fall apart into shiny heaps of junk kept coming off the assembly lines, things didn't go badly at first. Doyle says that on Edsel Day more than 6,500 Edsels were either ordered by or actually delivered to customers. That was a good showing, but there were isolated signs of resistance. For instance, a New England dealer selling Edsels in one showroom and Buicks in another reported that two prospects walked into the Edsel showroom, took a look at the Edsel, and placed orders for Buicks on the spot.

In the next few days, sales dropped sharply, but that was to be expected once the bloom was off. Automobile deliveries to dealers—one of the important indicators in the trade—are customarily measured in ten-day periods, and during the first ten days of September, on only six of which the Edsel was on sale, it racked up 4,095; this was lower than Doyle's first-day figure because many of the initial purchases were of models and color combinations not in stock, which had to be factory-assembled to order. The delivery total for the second ten-day period was off slightly, and that for the third was down to just under 3,600. For the first ten days of October, nine of which were business days, there were only 2,751 deliveries—an average of just over three hundred cars a day. In order to sell the 200,000 cars per year that would make the Edsel operation profitable the Ford Company would have to move an average of between six and seven hundred each business day—a good many more than three hundred a day. On the night of Sunday, October 13th, Ford put on a mammoth television spectacular for Edsel, pre-empting the time ordinarily allotted to the Ed Sullivan show, but though the program cost $400,000 and starred Bing Crosby and Frank Sinatra, it failed to cause any sharp spurt in sales. Now it was obvious that things were not going at all well.

Among the former executives of the Edsel Division, opinions differ as to the exact moment when the portents of doom became unmistakable. Krafve feels that the moment did not arrive until sometime late in October. Wallace, in his capacity as Edsel's pipe-smoking semi-Brain Truster, goes a step further by pinning the start of the disaster to a specific date—October 4th, the day the first Soviet sputnik went into orbit, shattering the myth of American technical pre-eminence and precipitating a public revulsion against Detroit's fancier baubles. Public Relations Director Warnock maintains that his barometric sensitivity to the public temper enabled him to call the turn as early as mid-September; contrariwise, Doyle says he maintained his optimism until mid-November, by which time he was about the only man in the division who had not concluded it would take a miracle to save the Edsel. "In November," says Wallace, sociologically, "there was panic, and its concomitant—mob action." The mob action took the form of a concerted tendency to blame the design of the car for the whole debacle; Edsel men who had previously had nothing but lavish praise for the radiator grille and rear end now went around muttering that any fool could see they were ludicrous. The obvious sacrificial victim was Brown, whose stock had gone through the roof at the time of the regally accoladed debut of his design, in August, 1955. Now, without having done anything further, for either better or worse, the poor fellow became the company scapegoat. "Beginning in November, nobody talked to Roy," Wallace says. On November 27th, as if things weren't bad enough, Charles Kreisler, who as the only Edsel dealer in Manhattan provided its prize showcase, announced that he was turning in his franchise because of poor sales, and it was rumored that he added, "The Ford Motor Company has laid an egg." He thereupon signed up with American Motors to sell its Rambler, which, as the only domestic small car then on the market, was already the possessor of a zooming sales curve. Doyle grimly commented that the Edsel Division was "not concerned" about Kreisler's defection.

By December, the panic at Edsel had abated to the point where its sponsors could pull themselves together and begin casting about for ways to get sales moving again. Henry Ford II, manifesting himself to Edsel dealers on closed-circuit television, urged them to remain calm, promised that the company would back them to the limit, and said flatly, "The Edsel is here to stay." A million and a half letters went out over Krafve's signature to owners of medium-priced cars, asking them to drop around at their local dealers and test-ride the Edsel; everyone doing so, Krafve promised, would be given an eight-inch plastic scale model of the car, whether he bought a full-size one or not. The Edsel

Division picked up the check for the scale models—a symptom of desperation indeed, for under normal circumstances no automobile manufacturer would make even a move to outfumble its dealers for such a tab. (Up to that time, the dealers had paid for everything, as is customary.) The division also began offering its dealers what it called "sales bonuses," which meant that the dealers could knock anything from one hundred to three hundred dollars off the price of each car without reducing their profit margin. Krafve told a reporter that sales up to then were about what he had expected them to be, although not what he had hoped they would be; in his zeal not to seem unpleasantly surprised, he appeared to be saying that he had expected the Edsel to fail. The Edsel's advertising campaign, which had started with studied dignity, began to sound a note of stridency. "Everyone who has seen it knows—with us—that the Edsel is a success," a magazine ad declared, and in a later ad this phrase was twice repeated, like an incantation: "The Edsel is a success. It is a new idea —a YOU idea—on the American Road. . . . The Edsel is a success." Soon the even less high-toned but more dependable advertising themes of price and social status began to intrude, in such sentences as "They'll know you've *arrived* when you drive up in an Edsel" and "The one that's really new is the lowest-priced, too!" In the more rarefied sectors of Madison Avenue, a resort to rhymed slogans is usually regarded as an indication of artistic depravity induced by commercial necessity.

From the frantic and costly measures the Edsel Division took in December, it garnered one tiny crumb: for the first ten-day period of 1958, it was able to report, sales were up 18.6 percent over those of the last ten days of 1957. The catch, as the *Wall Street Journal* alertly noted, was that the latter period embraced one more selling day than the earlier one, so, for practical purposes, there had scarcely been a gain at all. In any case, that early-January word of meretricious cheer turned out to be the Edsel Division's last gesture. On January 14,

1958, the Ford Motor Company announced that it was consolidating the Edsel Division with the Lincoln-Mercury Division to form a Mercury-Edsel-Lincoln Division, under the management of James J. Nance, who had been running Lincoln-Mercury. It was the first time that one of the major automobile companies had lumped three divisions into one since General Motors' merger of Buick, Oldsmobile, and Pontiac back in the depression, and to the people of the expunged Edsel Division the meaning of the administrative move was all too clear. "With that much competition in a division, the Edsel wasn't going anywhere," Doyle says. "It became a stepchild."

For the last year and ten months of its existence, the Edsel was very much a stepchild—generally neglected, little advertised, and kept alive only to avoid publicizing a boner any more than necessary and in the forlorn hope that it *might* go somewhere after all. What advertising it did get strove quixotically to assure the automobile trade that everything was dandy; in mid-February an ad in *Automotive News* had Nance saying,

> Since the formation of the new M-E-L Division at Ford Motor Company, we have analyzed with keen interest the sales progress of the Edsel. We think it is quite significant that during the five months since the Edsel was introduced, Edsel sales have been greater than the first five months' sales for any other new make of car ever introduced on the American Road. . . . Edsel's steady progress can be a source of satisfaction and a great incentive to all of us.

Nance's comparison, however, was almost meaningless, no new make ever having been introduced anything like so grandiosely, and the note of confidence could not help ringing hollow.

It is quite possible that Nance's attention was never called to an article by S. I. Hayakawa, the semanticist, that was published in the spring of 1958 in *ETC: A Review of General Semantics,* a quarterly magazine, under the title, "Why the Edsel Laid an Egg." Hayakawa, who is both the founder and the editor of *ETC,* explained in an introductory note that he considered the subject within the purview of general semantics because automobiles, like words, are "important . . . symbols in American culture," and went on to argue that the Edsel's flop could be attributed to Ford Company executives who had been "listening too long to the motivation-research people" and who, in their efforts to turn out a car that would satisfy customers' sexual fantasies and the like, had failed to supply reasonable and practical transportation, thereby neglecting "the reality principle." "What the motivation researchers failed to tell their clients . . . is that *only* the psychotic and the gravely neurotic *act out* their irrationalities and their compensatory fantasies," Hayakawa admonished Detroit briskly, and added, "The trouble with selling symbolic gratification via such expensive items as . . . the Edsel Hermaphrodite . . . is the competition offered by much cheaper forms of symbolic gratification, such as *Playboy* (fifty cents a copy), *Astounding Science Fiction* (thirty-five cents a copy), and television (free)."

Notwithstanding the competition from *Playboy,* or possibly because the symbol-motivated public included people who could afford both, the Edsel kept rolling—but just barely. The car moved, as salesmen say, though hardly at the touch of a toothpick. In fact, as a stepchild it sold about as well as it had sold as a favorite son, suggesting that all the hoopla, whether about symbolic gratification or mere horsepower, had had little effect one way or the other. The new Edsels that were registered with the motor-vehicle bureaus of the various states during 1958 numbered 34,481—considerably fewer than new cars of any competing make, and less than one-fifth of the 200,000 a year necessary if the Edsel was to show a profit, but still representing an investment by motorists of over a hundred million dollars. The picture actually brightened in November, 1958, with the advent of the Edsel's second-year models. Shorter by up to eight inches, lighter by up to five hundred pounds, and with engines less potent by as much as 158 horsepower, they had a price range running from five hundred to eight hundred dollars less than that of their predecessors. The vertical grille and the slant-eyed rear end were still there, but the modest power and proportions persuaded *Consumer Reports* to relent and say, "The Ford Motor Company, after giving last year's initial Edsel model a black eye, has made a respectable and even likable automobile of it." Quite a number of motorists seemed to agree; about two thousand more Edsels were sold in the first half of 1959 than had been sold in the first half of 1958, and by the early summer of 1959 the car was moving at the rate of around four thousand a month. Here, at last, was progress; sales were at almost a quarter of the minimum profitable rate, instead of a mere fifth.

On July 1, 1959, there were 83,849 Edsels on the country's roads. The largest number (8,344) were in California, which is beset with far and away the largest number of cars of practically all makes, and the smallest number were in Alaska, Vermont, and Hawaii (122, 119, and 110, respectively). All in all, the Edsel seemed to have found a niche for itself as an amusingly eccentric curiosity. Although the Ford Company, with its stockholders' money still disappearing week after week into the Edsel, and with small cars now clearly the order of the day, could scarcely affect a sentimental approach to the subject, it nonetheless took an outside chance and, in mid-October of 1959, brought out a third series of annual models. The 1960 Edsel appeared a little more than a month after the Falcon, Ford's first—and instantly successful—venture into the small-car field, and was scarcely an Edsel at all; gone were both the vertical grille and the horizontal rear end, and what remained looked like a cross between a Ford Fairlane and a Pontiac. Its initial sales were abysmal; by the middle of November only one plant—in Louisville, Kentucky—was still turning out Edsels, and it was turning out only about twenty a day. On November 19th, the Ford Foundation, which was planning to sell a block of its vast holdings of stock in the Ford Motor Company, issued the prospectus that is required by law under such circumstances, and stated therein, in a footnote to a section describing the company's products, that the Edsel had been "introduced in September 1957 and discontinued in November 1959." The same day, this mumbled admission was confirmed and amplified by a Ford Company spokesman, who did some mumbling of his own. "If we knew the reason people aren't buying the Edsel, we'd probably have done something about it," he said.

The final quantitative box score shows that from the beginning right up to November 19th, 110,810 Edsels were produced and 109,466 were sold. (The remaining 1,344, almost all of them 1960 models, were disposed of in short order with the help of drastic price cuts.) All told, only 2,846 of the 1960 Edsels were ever produced, making models of that year a potential collector's item. To be sure, 1960 Edsels are not as scarce as the Type 41 Bugatti, of which no more than eleven specimens were made, back in the late twenties, to be sold only to bona-fide kings, and the 1960 Edsel's reasons for being a rarity are not exactly as acceptable, socially or commercially, as the Type 41 Bugatti's. Still, a 1960-Edsel Owners' Club may yet appear.

The final fiscal box score on the Edsel fiasco will probably never be known, because the Ford Motor Company's public reports do not include breakdowns of gains and losses within the individual divisions. Financial buffs estimate, however, that the company lost something like $200 million on the Edsel after it appeared; add to this the officially announced expenditure of $250 million before it appeared, subtract about a hundred million invested in plant and equipment that were salvageable for other uses, and the net loss is $350 million. If these estimates are right, every Edsel the company manufactured cost it in lost money about $3,200, or about the price of another one. In other, harsher words, the company would have saved itself money if, back in 1955, it had decided not to produce the Edsel at all but simply to give away 110,810 specimens of its comparably priced car, the Mercury.

The end of the Edsel set off an orgy of gloating hindsight in the press. *Time* declared, "The Edsel was a classic case of the wrong car for the wrong market at the wrong time. It was also a prime example of the limitations of market research, with its 'depth interviews' and 'motivational' mumbo-jumbo." If *Time* had previously had any such ideas about either the Edsel or the spadework preceding its introduction, it had kept them to itself. *Business Week,* which shortly before the Edsel made its bow had described it with patent solemnity and apparent approval, now pronounced it "a nightmare" and appended a few pointedly critical remarks about Wallace's research, which was rapidly achieving a scapegoat status equal to that of Brown's design. (Jumping up and down on motivational research was, and is, splendid sport, but, of course, the implication that it dictated, or even influenced, the Edsel's design is entirely false, since the research, being intended only to provide a theme for advertising and promotion, was not undertaken until after Brown had completed his design.) The *Wall Street Journal*'s obituary of the Edsel made a point that was probably sounder, and certainly more original.

> Large corporations are often accused of rigging markets, administering prices, and otherwise dictating to the consumer [it observed]. And yesterday Ford Motor Company announced its two-year experiment with the medium-priced Edsel has come to an

> end . . . for want of buyers. All this is quite a ways from auto makers being able to rig markets or force consumers to take what they want them to take. . . . And the reason, simply, is that there is no accounting for tastes. . . . When it comes to dictating, the consumer is the dictator without peer.

The tone of the piece was friendly and sympathetic; the Ford Company, it seemed, had endeared itself to the *Journal* by playing the great American situation-comedy role of Daddy the Bungler.

As for the post-mortem explanations of the debacle that have been offered by former Edsel executives, they are notable for their reflective tone—something like that of a knocked-out prize fighter opening his eyes to find an announcer's microphone pushed into his face. In fact, Krafve, like many a flattened pugilist, blames his own bad timing; he contends that if he had been able to thwart the apparently immutable mechanics and economics of Detroit, and had somehow been able to bring out the Edsel in 1955, or even 1956, when the stock market and the medium-priced-car market were riding high, the car would have done well and would still be doing well. That is to say, if he had seen the punch coming, he would have ducked. Krafve refuses to go along with a sizable group of laymen who tend to attribute the collapse to the company's decision to call the car the Edsel instead of giving it a brisker, more singable name, reducible to a nickname other than "Ed" or "Eddie," and not freighted with dynastic connotations. As far as he can see, Krafve still says, the Edsel's name did not affect its fortunes one way or the other.

Brown agrees with Krafve that bad timing was the chief mistake. "I frankly feel that the styling of the automobile had very little, if anything, to do with its failure," he says, and his frankness may pretty safely be left unchallenged. "The Edsel program, like any other project planned for future markets, was based on the best information available at the time in which decisions were made. The road to Hell is paved with good intentions!"

Doyle, who has the born salesman's intensely personal feeling about his customers, talks like a man betrayed by a friend—the American public. "It was a buyers' strike," he says. "People weren't in the mood for the Edsel. Why not is a mystery to me. What they'd been buying for several years encouraged the industry to build exactly this kind of car. We gave it to them, and they wouldn't take it. Well, they shouldn't have acted like that. You can't just wake up somebody one day and say, 'That's enough, you've been running in the wrong direction.' Anyway, *why* did they do it? Golly, how the industry worked and worked over the years—getting rid of gear-shifting, providing interior comfort, providing plus performance for use in emergencies! And now the public wants these little beetles. I don't get it!"

Wallace's sputnik theory provides an answer to Doyle's question about why people weren't in the mood, and, furthermore, it is sufficiently cosmic to befit a semi-Brain Truster. It also leaves Wallace free to defend the validity of his motivational-research studies as of the time when they were conducted. "I don't think we yet know the depths of the psychological effect that that first orbiting had on us all," he says. "Somebody had beaten us to an important gain in technology, and immediately people started writing articles about how crummy Detroit products were, particularly the heavily ornamented and status-symbolic medium-priced cars. In 1958, when none of the small cars were out except the Rambler, Chevy almost ran away with the market, because it had the simplest car. The American people had put themselves on a self-imposed austerity program. Not buying Edsels was their hair shirt."

To any relics of the sink-or-swim nineteenth-century days of American industry, it must seem strange that Wallace can afford to puff on his pipe and analyze the holocaust so amiably. The obvious point of the Edsel's story is the defeat of a giant motor company, but what is just as surprising is that the giant did not come apart, or even get seriously hurt in the fall, and neither did the majority of the people who went down with him. Owing largely to the success of four of its other cars—the Ford, the Thunderbird, and, more recently, the small Falcon and Comet—the Ford Company, as an investment, has survived gloriously. True, it had a bad time of it in 1958, when, partly because of the Edsel, net income per share of its stock fell from $5.40 to $2.12, dividends per share from $2.40 to $2.00, and the market price of its stock from a 1957 high of about $60 to a 1958 low of under $40. But all these losses were more than recouped in 1959, when net income per share was $8.24, dividends per share were $2.80, and the price of the stock reached a high of around $90. In 1960 and 1961, things went even better. So the 280,000 Ford stockholders listed on the books in 1957 have had little to complain about unless they sold at the height of the panic. On the other hand, six thousand white-collar workers were squeezed out of their jobs as a result of the Mercury-Edsel-Lincoln consolidation, and the average number of Ford employees fell from 191,759 in 1957 to 142,076 the following year, climbing back to only 159,541 in 1959. And, of course, dealers who gave up profitable franchises in other makes and then went broke trying to sell Edsels aren't likely to be very cheerful about the experience. Under the terms of the consolidation of the Lincoln-Mercury and Edsel Divisions, most of the agencies for the three makes were consolidated, too. In the consolidation, some Edsel dealers were squeezed out, and it can have been small comfort to those of them who went bankrupt to learn later that when the Ford Company finally discontinued making the car, it agreed to pay those of their former colleagues who had weathered the crisis one-half of the original cost of their Edsel signs, and was granting them substantial rebates on all Edsels in stock at the time of discontinuance. Still, automobile dealers, some of whom work on credit margins as slim as those of Miami hotel operators, occasionally go broke with even the most popular cars. And among those who earn their living in the rough-and-tumble world of automobile salesrooms, where Detroit is not always spoken of with affection, many will concede that the Ford Company, once it had found itself stuck with a lemon, did as much as it reasonably could to bolster dealers who had cast their lot with Edsel. A spokesman for the National Automobile Dealers Association has since stated, "So far as we know, the Edsel dealers were generally satisfied with the way they were treated."

Foote, Cone & Belding also ended up losing money on the Edsel account, since its advertising commissions did not entirely compensate for the extraordinary expense it had gone to of hiring sixty new people and opening up a posh office in Detroit. But its losses were hardly irreparable; the minute there were no more Edsels to advertise, it was hired to advertise Lincolns, and although that arrangement did not last very long, the firm has happily survived to sing the praises of such clients as General Foods, Lever Brothers, and Trans World Airways. A rather touching symbol of the loyalty that the agency's employees have for its former client is the fact that on every workday its private parking lot in Chicago is still dotted with Edsels. These faithful drivers, incidentally, are not unique. If Edsel owners have not found the means to a dream fulfillment, and if some of them for a while had to put up with harrowing mechanical disorders, many of them cherish their cars as if they were Confederate bills, and the market in used Edsels is still firm, with few cars being offered.

By and large, the former Edsel executives did not just land on their feet, they landed in clover. Certainly no one can accuse the Ford Company of giving vent to its chagrin in the old-fashioned way, by vulgarly causing heads to roll. Krafve was assigned to assist Robert S. McNamara, at that time a Ford divisional vice-president (and more recently, of course, Secretary of Defense), for a couple of months, and then he moved to a staff job in company headquarters, stayed there for about a year, and left to become a vice-president of the Raytheon Company, of Waltham, Massachusetts, a leading electronics firm. In April, 1960, he was made its president. Doyle, too, was offered a staff job with Ford, but after taking a trip abroad to think it over he decided to retire. "It was a question of my relationship to my dealers," he explains. "I had assured them that the company was fully behind the Edsel for keeps, and I didn't feel that I was the fellow to tell them now that it wasn't." After his retirement, Doyle remained about as busy as ever, keeping an eye on various businesses in which he has set up various friends and relatives, and conducting a consulting business of his own in Detroit. About a month before Edsel's consolidation with Mercury and Lincoln, Warnock, the publicity man, left the division to become director of news services for the International Telephone & Telegraph Corp., in New York—a position he left in June, 1960, to become vice-president of Communications Counselors, the public-relations arm of McCann-Erickson. Brown, the embattled stylist, stayed on in Detroit for a while as chief stylist of Ford commercial vehicles and then went with the Ford Motor Company, Ltd., of England, where, again as chief stylist, he was assigned to direct the design of Consuls, Anglias, trucks, and tractors. He insisted that this post didn't represent the Ford version of Siberia. "I have found it to be a most satisfying experience, and one of the best steps I have ever taken in my . . . career," he stated firmly in a letter from England. "We are building a styling office and a styling team second to none in Europe." Wallace, the semi-Brain Truster, was asked to continue semi-Brain Trusting for Ford, and, since he still didn't like living in Detroit, or near it, was permitted to move to New York and to spend only two days a week at headquarters. ("They didn't seem to care any more where I operated from," he says modestly.) At the end of 1958, he left Ford, and he has since finally achieved his heart's desire—to become a full-time academic. He set about getting a doctorate in sociology at Columbia, writing his thesis on social change in Westport, Connecticut, which he investigated by busily quizzing its inhabitants; meanwhile, he taught a course on "The Dynamics of Social Behavior" at the New School for Social Research, in Greenwich Village. "I'm through with industry," he was heard to declare one day, with evident satisfaction, as he boarded a train for Westport, a bundle of questionnaires under his arm. Early in 1962, he became Dr. Wallace.

The present euphoria of these former Edsel men does not stem entirely from the fact of their economic survival; they appear to have been enriched spiritually. They are inclined to speak of their Edsel experience—except for those still with Ford, who are inclined to speak of it as little as possible—with the verve and garrulity of old comrades-in-arms hashing over their most thrilling campaign. Doyle is perhaps the most passionate reminiscer in the group. "It was more fun than I've ever had before or since," he told a caller in 1960. "I suppose that's because I worked the hardest ever. We all did. It was a good crew. The people who came with Edsel knew they were taking a chance, and I like people who'll take chances. Yes, it was a wonderful experience, in spite of the unfortunate thing that happened. And we were on the right track, too! When I went to Europe just before retiring, I saw how it is there—nothing but compact cars, yet they've still got traffic jams over there, they've still got parking problems, they've still got accidents. Just try getting in and out of those low taxicabs without hitting your head, or try not to get clipped while you're walking around the Arc de Triomphe. This small-car thing won't last forever. I can't see American drivers being satisfied for long with manual gear-shifting and limited performance. The pendulum will swing back."

Warnock, like many a public-relations man before him, claims that his job gave him an ulcer—his second. "But I got over it," he says. "That great Edsel team—I'd just like to see what it could have done if it had had the right product at the right time. It could have made millions, that's what! The whole thing was two years out of my life that I'll never forget. It was history in the making. Doesn't it all tell you something about America in the fifties—high hopes, and less than complete fulfillment of them?"

Krafve, the boss of the great team *manqué,* is entirely prepared to testify that there is more to his former subordinates' talk than just the romantic vaporings of old soldiers. "It was a wonderful group to work with," he said not long ago. "They really put their hearts and guts into the job. I'm interested in a crew that's strongly motivated, and that one was. When things went bad, the Edsel boys could have cried about how they'd given up wonderful opportunities to come with us, but if anybody did, I never heard about it. I'm not surprised that they've mostly come out all right. In industry, you take a bump now and then, but you bounce back as long as you don't get defeated inside. I like to get together with somebody once in a while—Gayle Warnock or one of the others—and go over the humorous incidents, the tragic incidents. . . ."

Whether the nostalgia of the Edsel boys for the Edsel runs to the humorous or to the tragic, it is a thought-provoking phenomenon. Maybe it means merely that they miss the limelight they first basked in and later squirmed in, or maybe it means that a time has come when—as in Elizabethan drama but seldom before in American business—failure can have a certain grandeur that success never knows.

3 / A Proust in Wall Street

WALTER KNOWLTON GUTMAN, a former professional art critic and a current member in good standing of the New York Society of Security Analysts, who once described himself in an article published by the magazine *Investor* as "a Proust in Wall Street," is probably the only writer of a broker's stock-market letter whose readers count on him not only for financial advice but also for cultural commentary, psychological insights, and even spiritual guidance. In appearance, Gutman's letter—a stenciled weekly affair that runs anywhere from eight hundred to fifteen hundred words and is mailed out (until recently, free of charge) to several thousand customers and potential customers of the brokerage and investment-banking firm for which he works—is much like the weekly letters issued by dozens of brokerage firms. It is basically a tip sheet, designed to stimulate his employer's business. What is far less usual is the intensity of the relationship between writer and reader that Gutman's letter establishes and maintains. This intensity is reflected in the severe withdrawal symptoms that some readers manifest when they are suddenly deprived of it—as thousands were several years ago, when Gutman, who had been writing for the brokerage firm of Goodbody & Company for nine years, moved over to Shields & Company. As the Goodbody customers gradually learned the address of their oracle's new shrine, many of them wrote to Gutman pleading to be put on the mailing list for his new letter. Gutman, almost certainly the only security analyst with fans who address him by his first name, as if he were a television performer, received the following communication from a reader in Shreveport, Louisiana: "Dear Walter: I have wondered where you went, and, thank God, I've finally located you." Another addict, a resident of both Dallas and Memphis, adopted an almost suppliant tone, writing humbly, "Mr. Gutman, I want to tell you how much an admirer I have been of yours. . . . I miss your letters so very much now that you are with another firm. You have been so very right about the steels." Understandably touched, Gutman had the Dallas-Memphis man added to the Shields mailing list, where he remained for several months—or until the firm's partners decided to take him off again, since he had not bought or sold any stocks. The Shields action brought a quick reaction. Not only did the Southerner, in a special-delivery letter, butter up Gutman ("There is a lot of consolation in reading your letter" and "I think you are the greatest security analyst in the whole U.S.A.") but, evidently suspecting the cause of his disbarment, he enclosed an order for a hundred shares of American Telephone & Telegraph. Since a hundred shares of A.T.&T. then cost about $22,-000, plus a $61 broker's commission, there is reason to believe that, when pressed, people will sign up for the free letter at a subscription rate that would be the envy of other periodicals.

The weekly essay that inspires such devotion (currently composed on behalf of Stearns & Company) is, as a rule, a slightly haphazard amalgam of spontaneous remarks about whatever happens to be on Gutman's mind at the moment of creation and shrewd investment suggestions—that is to say, tips. Not long ago, for example, he opened a letter with a discussion of atomic-particle accelerators, sidled easily over to the subject of demonism and science, sloped off into Zen Buddhism, paused to speculate about the influence of the beat group of writers on American foreign policy, and then, a trifle abruptly, recommended the stock of a British pharmaceutical company that had found a promising new treatment for athlete's foot. Some of Gutman's readers seem more interested in the preliminaries than in the fiscal punch lines, and once one of these, an investor in Lowell, Massachusetts, who had tracked him down at Shields, wrote him, in a bemused style quite characteristic of Gutman fans, "Needless to say, your philosophical, historical, and scientific observations have been very stimulating in a sort of semi-physical sense."

To Gutman, such a response is highly gratifying. A heavy-set, jowly, diffident man in his fifties, whose habitual expression approximates the tentative smile of an apprehensive infant, and who usually speaks in a half-audible mumble, he has, in less exalted moods than the one in which he compared himself to Proust, referred to himself as a frustrated writer (sometimes, either inadvertently or wistfully, he speaks of the investment firm that employs him as "my publishers"), and he has admitted that he would rather think of a good phrase for his letter than make a quick five hundred dollars on a stock trade. It might be supposed that his digressive, not to say offhand, manner of dishing out investment advice would alienate those customers who are interested in nothing more rarefied than buying cheap and selling dear, but this does not seem to have occurred, and the reason may well be that when Gutman finally gets down to recommendations and predictions, they are likely to be valid. To give two striking examples, in November, 1957, taking a totally divergent line from most financial seers, he forecast that the next bull market would be in bonds, and in March, 1958, when the stock market was seriously depressed and most pundits were saying that it would go lower, he declared in a letter that he thought the Dow-Jones industrial average would reach record highs before the year was out. Both predictions came triumphantly true. "In recent years, when I've been notably right about the market a few times, the literary quality of my letters hasn't been commented on quite so much," Gutman has remarked resignedly. "But no matter what, I try to write with rhythm and drama." These days, the general feeling among his employers—and even among his most hard-boiled readers, who, if they were faithfully following his investment suggestions at the time of the market crash of May, 1962, got considerably bloodied as a result—seems to be that as long as he continues to be right enough of the time, they will defend to the death his entitlement to all the rhythm and drama he wants.

Of the uncounted and uncountable tons of reading matter (or, to use the technical term, "literature") that brokerage houses pour out in a steady cascade, weekly market letters are only a part. There are also statistical compilations of various sorts and special reports on individual companies, as well as year-end letters, monthly letters, bimonthly letters, fortnightly letters, and even daily letters, not to mention letters issued at irregular intervals, when the writer feels that he has something to say. (One downtown author, Gerald M. Loeb, of E. F. Hutton & Company, used to crank out two letters a day—a morning one and an afternoon one—but lately he has joined the more relaxed circle of those who compose at the dictates not of the calendar or the clock but of the creative fit. Loeb deplores the fact that there are very few energetic young men in Wall Street these days who are willing to get up early enough in the morning to have a letter ready for distribution by 10 A.M., when the Stock Exchange opens; he takes this to be a sign that the Street is getting soft.) Whatever their frequency, market letters as a group are scarcely fascinating reading, except to a truly economic man; half a day spent going through a sheaf of them tends to leave the common reader feeling as if he had been hit, not hard but repeatedly, with a blunt instrument. This effect is not entirely unintentional. Most letter writers pride themselves on sticking strictly to business, and entertainment value is something that they achieve only inadvertently—as when a man who has guessed wrong comes up with a solemn essay on the advantages of "scientific loss-taking."

Practically alone among writers of market letters, Gutman sets out quite advertently to entertain. "A successful letter does not depend so much on being right as on being interesting," he says. "The clientele is remarkably charitable about error." Although now and then he turns out a letter that is as relentlessly statistical and businesslike as the next firm's, he usually chats away as the spirit moves him, and in the decade or so that he has been writing letters he has touched on, among many other things, the fact that the first Queen Elizabeth was once worried for fear an oak shortage would force her to retrench on her shipbuilding program; the comeback appearance, some years ago, of Judy Garland at the Palace Theatre; "the lonesomeness of the past"; the fact that Lord Nelson's flagship, the *Victory,* was a century old at the time of the Battle of Trafalgar; the dancers and drummers at the Katherine Dunham School; a notion of his that "copper is the metal of a passionate world"; love ("The earth now has on its surface about two billion people who either are or have been lovers. But despite their vast experience, they still want to hear about it"); and the early culture of Canaan. Gutman has a predilection for historical references—he once managed to work Pericles, Alexander, Julius Caesar, Genghis Khan, Columbus, and George Washington into a single letter—and for such illuminations as "What makes a farsighted man is an ability both to believe in and to accurately gauge the shadow world of possibility; what makes a foolish gambler is an unfortunate lack of accuracy attached to a real belief. As the shadow world turns into the statistical world, fortunes are made." (The letter to which this passage provided the climax brought a particularly enthusiastic response from readers, in the form of both congratulatory messages and orders to buy stocks.)

Gutman is also fond of "psychoanalyzing the market," as he puts it. "I called the 1949 rise in stock prices by using Freudian analysis," he recalls. "I figured women would go on buying things, because their psychological necessity, unlike that of men, didn't require them to sell in the expectation of an economically orthodox postwar depression." In the summer of 1958, in the second letter he wrote for Shields, he gave his new readers an inkling of what was in store for them by sending out a composition headed "A Psychoanalysis of War and Inflation." "A terror dream, while frightening, is less frightening than real fears," this letter said, in part. "In the past, our worries about inflation have been a type of terror dream, taking the minds of our leaders off their real problems. In a country as economically powerful as ours, there is never any reason to be deeply concerned about inflation except during times of war. But fear of inflation represents a safe sort of shiver." Even when Gutman isn't actually psychoanalyzing anything, he sometimes drops into psychological jargon. "Take the High Voltage Engineering Corporation . . . a favorite of mine," he said in one letter, and then asked musingly, "Am I . . . overestimating the value of the loved object?" At cocktail parties in Westport, where he has lived over most of the past decade or so, Gutman sometimes describes himself to new acquaintances as an analyst—a perfectly accurate term, of course, since in the quaint old streets south of Fulton an analyst is still a student of securities—and if he is then asked about repressions and complexes, he doesn't mind in the least.

Gutman is fully aware that, market-letter writing being the traditional, formal métier it is, he is getting away with murder, and he is inclined to adduce this fact as evidence in support of a pet theory of his—that under Wall Street's silk vest beats a liberal heart, eager to defend freedom of expression on behalf of anyone who demands it. By way of a concrete example, he cites his Judy Garland letter, written in December, 1951, in which he took up about four-fifths of his space with a paean to the actress's courage and determination, and only then buckled down to a recommendation for Corning Glass common. "In a way, you have to admire the Goodbody partners for allowing me to use Judy Garland as a stock-market theme," Gutman has since observed. As even a casual student of his prose will admit, you have to admire them for more than that. Both Goodbody and Shields require that market letters on their letterheads be read by at least one partner before they go out, but in dealing with Gutman's writings both firms have for the most part maintained a hands-off policy. Indeed, in their anxiety not to interfere, the partners have often let stand the errors in spelling and syntax that Gutman, a highly impulsive writer, is prone to. (For example, the Goodbody partners were apparently content to let Gutman drop both ends of an orthographic double-header by spelling Genghis Khan "Ghengis Kahn.") In the realm of politics, Gutman, a Democrat, has been allowed such abrupt comments as "Hoover was an exceedingly opaque President" and "There hasn't been a good Republican in the White House since McKinley" (some of his colleagues take it as a sign of perversity that he stands up for McKinley), as well as numerous flattering references to Franklin D. Roosevelt. Of course, it cannot be assumed that all the powers at Goodbody, Shields or Stearns have gritted their teeth whenever Gutman expressed an anti-Republican sentiment—those firms, as a matter of fact, number Democrats among their partners—but surely the Goodbody bosses deserve some sort of civil-liberties medal for allowing Gutman, in May, 1958, to discuss the drinking habits of the late John L. Goodbody, who had been a partner in the firm until his death, in 1951, and has since become one of its household gods. "John L. was as nearly a Gargantuan character as this writer has actually met," declared Gutman admiringly. "The phrase 'pour it down' was not a literary exaggeration when applied to John L.; it was a statistical description." As it happened, Gutman left Goodbody & Company a couple of months after that, but it was on his own initiative, and the partners told him they were very sorry to see him go.

Speaking of another letter of his, Gutman, who has retained much of the vocabulary he learned as an art critic, said a while ago, "That was a good one, because the separate thoughts, like different metals, had been fused by an emotion." In the letter in question, he told about a ride he had taken in a white Cadillac along Avenue B, in the Lower East Side of Manhattan, remarked on the paradox of poverty in the midst of wealth, and then plunged into an exegesis of the relationship between dreams and reality. Gutman's comment on the letter suggests the basic stylistic problem posed by his method of writing; namely, how to fuse his "separate thoughts" with his stock-market recommendations. He admits that he often takes off on his philosophical flights without having the faintest idea how he is going to get down to the hard ground of Wall Street, and certainly some of his landings have been less smooth than others. In the case of the antiquity of Nelson's ship, there was no problem, since the point of the preamble was that technology is moving faster than it used to, which led quite naturally into plugs for Fansteel Metallurgical and Kawecki Chemical. The Judy Garland letter was another matter. Here Gutman had to use all his literary guile to get safely back to earth. He accomplished the feat, more or less, by drawing a parallel between Miss Garland and the average investor—both, in his view, embattled souls struggling on against odds—and then slipping into his Corning Glass commercial. A bumpy landing, perhaps, but a gallant one.

After Gutman moved to Shields, his transitions tended to become more abrupt, possibly because his preliminary essays began wandering more widely. Near the top of page 2 of his science-demonism-Zen-foreign-policy letter, he was observing, "For a while, science passed out of the power of the demons and into a time of apparently sure knowledge. But as it delved into the inner forces of life, the demons re-entered." A dozen lines further along, he was into Zen and the beats, and was simultaneously running down the contemporary French philosophical writers: "Sartre and Camus are great, but they are locked in a sort of regret. The beat people are not locked in regret." Nor, the clientele of Shields was learning a couple of paragraphs later, were the makers of United States policy:

> It is possible that the whole nation is going beat. . . . Logically we shouldn't be allowing the Russians to be getting where they are, but if life were logical, there would be neither God nor demons in it. . . . Investors should try to make up their minds whether America will become more beat or more logical. . . . America has always been a profoundly instinctive country—we have always been much better at feeling than thinking; perhaps there is something to be gained by seeing some relationship between what is going on in art and among the beat generation to what is going on in our major national policies.

Finding himself part way down page 3 when that thought was delivered, Gutman simply threw up his hands and wrote, "But we have to make money in the meantime," and went on to plug his athlete's-foot-remedy company, Glaxo Laboratories. It was, Gutman admits, a failure of literary resourcefulness, but since Glaxo stock showed a satisfactory rise over the following weeks, nobody had much reason to complain, except perhaps Camus and Sartre, and Gutman made handsome amends to them a month later, when he wrote a letter entitled "The Challenge of Camus and the Berlin Crisis." In this, he laid down the flat, unhedged judgment that, locked in regret or not, the two Frenchmen are the greatest philosophical writers of our time.

More recently, Gutman has been writing his letter for Stearns & Company, which has altered the policy of his previous employers by insisting that recipients pay a fifty-dollar annual subscription fee for it unless they maintain sufficiently active brokerage accounts and thus earn it by paying stock commissions. On the evidence, Gutman's style has not been cramped by the setting of a price on his prose. Nor, it must be admitted, has he found a final solution to his problem of literary transitions. Rambling on about space travel in a letter of early 1962, he quoted a General Electric scientist as having declared that it is technically feasible to divert a small planet-like natural body called an asteroid in such a way that it could be used as a weapon against an earthly enemy. "I don't know how many asteroids there are," Gutman ruminated.

> I suppose I could find out by calling up the Planetarium—but this is a sort of gloomy Monday and I prefer to think that there are plenty of asteroids for everyone. Let's not get into a brushfire war with comet tails. But now I come to my idea: in order to escape from the asteroid the inhabitants of the doomed continent could simply attach a few rocket nozzles to the earth and away we'd go, dodging through the universe—this would upset all the sundials but we wouldn't be thinking of communism any more. When I originally thought of this was in connection with the togetherness movement. It seemed to me that it's pretty useless to send out a few astronauts to explore the universe and get back a billion years from now. I felt that beyond limited local explorations in the neighborhood of Venus and other planets we should all go. Make the earth into a rocket.

Three far-out pages later, Gutman still hadn't buckled down to business. "As to the stock market," he wrote abruptly, "all the domestic facts are pretty well known. There doesn't seem to be any strong ticker tape fantasy right now. I don't expect one next week. Rather dull, isn't it?"

Far afield as Gutman's own literary excursions sometimes take him, he can become extremely philosophical without budging from his home grounds of Wall Street. In this, too, he is atypical. Whatever other princely qualities—prudence, daring, probity, energy, diligence, suavity—Wall Streeters as a group may be said to possess, they are seldom thought of as being long on self-conscious awareness of their professional world as a social milieu. Gutman, however, has this quality in abundance, and will deliver homilies on the Street at the drop of a hat. At one time or another—in his letters, in conversation, in the articles he sometimes writes for financial magazines—he has uncorked such arresting remarks as "A brokerage-house board room is basically an adult recreation center," "Wall Street attracts neurotics because it is a dream world where you can leave a situation flat, without human complications, by simply selling out," "Stocks are jesters in the court of capitalism; what they say is true, but . . . when the stock markets go crazy, the kings of capitalism say 'hush,' " "The world of Wall Street is not different in a philosophic sense from the world of Toulouse-Lautrec," "People who are sensuous, who have a great deal of feeling for physical existence, don't particularly like or understand Wall Street; it's quite an abstract place," and (a recurring Gutman theme, like the phrase from Vinteuil's sonata in *Swann's Way*) "Basically, the stock market is feminine." In explaining the stock market's gender, Gutman has said, "The reason the board-room chairs are filled with tensely interested men is the possibility, always present, that the unexpected will happen, a mystery be revealed. There is nothing like the ticker tape except a woman—nothing that promises, hour after hour, day after day, such sudden exciting developments, nothing that disappoints so often or occasionally fulfills with such unbelievable, passionate magnificence." Besides feeling that there is nothing like a dame except ticker tape, Gutman is convinced that the historical relationship between Wall Street and women customers is a recapitulation of a growing and finally maturing relationship between one man and one woman. One recent evening, he developed this theory for a friend by saying, in his usual mumble, "At first, there was the stage in which women were considered a nuisance. Brokers didn't want them around, and sometimes wouldn't even accept them as customers. Then came the glittery-eyed stage, during which Wall Street thought it sensed a passive victim, and tried to have its way at women's expense. Now we are in the mature, tender stage, in which Wall Street realizes that it had better be good to women. The full implications of this, by the way, have not yet saturated industry, but they will."

As a onetime art critic and, more recently, a part-time painter himself, Gutman has a quite natural tendency to combine his two interests—finance and art. "Minnesota Mining & Manufacturing Company probably is entitled to be called the Picasso of industry," he wrote in one article, going on to explain, lucidly enough, "Picasso saw the possibilities of Cubism the way the managers of Three-M saw the possibilities of adhesives." He has also occasionally had an opportunity to combine art and finance in a more practical way, by using his stock-market shrewdness to finance purchases from his painter friends. Some of the latter have shown a knack for driving bargains that Gutman views with both approval and astonishment. At the opening of a one-man show on Fifty-seventh Street a few years ago, he fell into conversation with a young girl who was a friend of the artist, and, while sipping a ceremonial Martini, told her that he would agree to buy one of the artist's paintings if a certain stock that he was interested in, then selling at about forty-five dollars a share, went up to seventy-five. "How about a small drawing if it hits fifty?" the young lady asked quickly. After some haggling, Gutman agreed to a drawing at fifty-five and a painting at seventy-five. The stock went to fifty-five, Gutman bought a drawing, and art and commerce benefited together.

In common with many other financiers, Gutman believes that money-making is itself something of an art, but he deviates from the orthodox version of this cozy doctrine in two particulars: first, he maintains that, except in rare cases, money-making is a rather low art form, on the order of soap sculpture, and, second, he flatly rejects the Wall Street dogma that stock-market fortunes are ordinarily the fruit not only of talent but of hard work. "Shortly before he died, old Marcus Goodbody, John L.'s brother, put the thing to me beautifully," Gutman recalled recently. "He was a unique character in Wall Street. We had a dark, shadowy library where I used to do research. One evening, just after I started working for Goodbody, an old man came into the library and wandered around the filing cabinets and shelves. I hadn't met him, and I didn't know who he was. He had a vague and dreamy look, like an artist, and since he had bushy eyebrows, it occurred to me that he might be related to Alfred Stieglitz, who, I knew, had relatives in Wall Street. Well, we got to talking, and I soon found out he was Marcus Goodbody. After a while, he asked me, 'Why haven't you more money?' I replied, 'Probably because I don't work hard enough.' He shook his old head and said, 'If you're going to make money, you won't work any harder than someone who doesn't make it.' Marcus should have known, and I say he was right. If you are going to make a fortune, you will see signs of doing it fairly quickly; otherwise you won't do it, or at least the probabilities are against you. Fortune-making is an art—there is a great deal about it that can't be explained, or anyway not in the simple, rational way that people like things explained—and, like any art, it must absorb your interest intensely. People who make fortunes are either intensely interested in their occupation, which only incidentally brings them a fortune, or intensely interested in money, or else there is a combination of those intensities. At any rate, intensity is part of the situation. Real money-makers hate to lose. Say what you will about the cool gambler who takes his losses without the flicker of an eyebrow—if this gambler has a real zest for the gold, he is planning how to get that money back. Behind that cool mask there is an inner sorrow and rage, produced by the traumatic experience of losing. I have seen money-makers lambaste someone whose advice has led to a loss. A money-maker cannot take a loss gracefully. As for me, I don't have the intense drive that's required. Oh, I've made money. During the mid-fifties, when I made more than I had ever thought of making, it came easily—no trouble at all. Maybe I felt that making it was pretty low-grade. Of course, if everybody could make money easily, we would have the economic millennium—humanity would escape from hard labor. But basically I consider making money for its own sake a rather poor sort of activity. Or do I? Sometimes I wonder. I *think* I do, but then maybe unconsciously I don't."

Effortless though Gutman's ascent to money-making may have been, it took him a long time. For some thirty years, he oscillated uncertainly between art and commerce, and it was only about ten years ago that he learned to fit them both into his life. His grandparents were Jewish immigrants from Germany; his father was a businessman, and his mother an enthusiastic amateur artist. Walter, an only child, was born in Chicago in 1903, and went to a pioneering progressive school there. When he was eleven, the family moved to New York, where the father set up a cotton-converting firm called Eugene Gutman & Company, and the son went to Horace Mann School. According to Harry Steeger, the president of Popular Publications, Inc., who was one of Walter's classmates at Horace Mann and has remained his friend ever since, Gutman as a schoolboy was already amazingly analytical. "Wally put everything on the end of a needle," Steeger says. "It almost drove his father crazy. Eugene Gutman was a simple, straightforward businessman. He'd make some plain statement about, say, the political situation, and Wally would turn it around, toss it up in the air, and play with it until his father was shouting with rage. Wally wanted everybody else to be analytical, too. He thought that was the road to salvation. One afternoon, he came over to our house—we were neighbors, in the West Eighties—and my mother happened to remark that she was bored. Wally piped up, 'Why not study something? That's the way to avoid boredom.' He took a fast look around the room, and then he went on, 'How about a doorknob? Why don't you study that doorknob over there until you know all there is to know about doorknobs?' "

It was Steeger who persuaded Eugene Gutman that after Horace Mann his son ought to go to college, rather than straight into the cotton-converting business. Walter went through Bowdoin in three years, editing the literary magazine and just scraping by in his required economics courses, and took his degree in 1924, with high honors in English. After graduation, he served a stint as a clerk in the family firm, but he showed so little talent that in a matter of weeks his father was ready to concede that he would never be a cotton converter. In the middle twenties, Eugene Gutman & Company was thriving, and for several years Walter was able to play the prodigal son, with his father's blessing. Between trips to France and Italy, where he visited art galleries, he studied for an M.A. in English at Yale, but he finally gave it up as a bad job. In the autumn of 1927, having resolved to begin supporting himself, he returned to New York and moved into the Henry Street Settlement, where young men received cheap quarters in exchange for two hours of social work a week, and soon he was contributing critical articles on such painters as John Sloan, Raphael Soyer, and George Bellows to the *Nation,* the *New Republic, Art in America,* and other magazines. Eventually, he became a regular contributor to *Creative Art,* a monthly published by Albert and Charles Boni, for which he wrote a column of news and gossip about the art world. By January, 1930, he had become well enough known to be one of the subjects chosen for a special exhibition entitled "The Critics Hung by Contemporary American Artists" and consisting of portraits of ten prominent art writers by prominent painters. Paul Kovner painted Gutman, who did not appreciate the result. "Purely conventional," he says.

However soul-satisfying such renown may have been, Gutman found art writing pretty unrewarding financially, and to supplement his income he began soliciting advertisements for *Creative Art,* speculating in the stock market with a few thousand dollars his father had turned over to him, and trying to sell the stock of Cities Service Corporation door to door. The *Creative Art* ads went fairly well, but the results of his speculations were mixed, and he never succeeded in unloading a single share of Cities Service, so his debut as a financial entrepreneur was not precisely auspicious. In 1929, he became involved in a new publishing venture in partnership with Steeger, who had already put in a successful stint as editor of a literary magazine called *Famous Story.* The new venture, an art magazine, lasted about four issues, and is remembered by its two proprietors because in one of the issues they transposed paragraphs of two articles by museum curators. The curatorial wrath called down on their heads is the single, melancholy bit of flotsam to mark where the magazine sank; Gutman can't remember anything else about it—not even what it was called—and neither can Steeger.

F. Scott Fitzgerald once wrote that there are no second acts in

American lives, but it can be argued that in the lives of many thousands of Americans of Fitzgerald's generation, and Gutman's, there have been not only second acts but second acts that began simultaneously —in the autumn of 1929. After the stock-market crash, Eugene Gutman & Company rapidly skidded to the brink of failure, and the crisis in the firm's affairs forced Mr. Gutman into virtual retirement (he died in 1939) and his son into finance. While still contributing regularly to *Creative Art,* Walter began to spend much of his time in the offices of Hentz & Company, at 60 Beaver Street, studying the stock market and trying to recover some of the family fortune by investing what remained of his father's money. "It wasn't as much of a change for him as you might think," Steeger has said. "It was just switching from analyzing paintings to analyzing stocks." Nevertheless, the years after 1929 were hardly a favorable time for that sort of change. The second and third phases of the crash, in 1932 and 1933, almost administered the *coup de grâce* to the Gutman fortune, but somehow Walter survived those years without actually going broke, and he found the experience both exciting and educational. "Wall Street in the depression years was like Cape Cod in September," he has said. "It was a place of past pleasure and revelry, now almost deserted, and racked by hurricanes. Those selling waves in the early thirties were truly like hurricanes. Everybody tried to look quiet and composed, but each of us knew what the others were thinking about—this unbelievable, immeasurable force, which might destroy us at any moment." Early in 1933, the immeasurable force hit *Creative Art,* which folded (the Bonis gave their news-and-gossip writer a set of Proust as a farewell present, never suspecting that it would launch him on a new career), and Gutman began devoting his full time to finance. The economic weather brightened somewhat in 1934, and that year he married Dorothy Darrow, the sister of Whitney Darrow, Jr., the cartoonist. The couple, who have since been divorced, took a small apartment at 26

Jones Street, in Greenwich Village, bought an old farmhouse in Hattertown, Connecticut, and spent the remainder of the thirties rocking along in the modest circumstances that, in those distant times, were pretty much the rule for people whose livings derived from Wall Street.

In the weeks after Pearl Harbor, there was still another market crash, and Gutman, who now had two children as well as a wife to support and was getting tired of being at the mercy of economic hurricanes, decided that he wanted a job. To this end, he spent his evenings studying statistics and security analysis at N.Y.U. The elderly beginner (he was now thirty-eight) was so anxious to have a position with a salary that he accepted one without any; in December, 1942, Goodbody & Company consented to take him on as a junior security analyst on a no-pay trial basis. The firm began paying him a month later, and kept it up regularly for fifteen and a half years. During Gutman's first years with Goodbody, his job was to make studies of individual companies, chiefly in the steel and chemical industries, and to write up his findings, salting them with advice on whether or not to buy the companies' stocks. In this capacity, he was able to keep up his habit of learning through market crashes. Shortly after the 1946 crash, his quest led him to the now defunct Jefferson School of Social Science, at Sixth Avenue and Fifteenth Street, which was generally considered to be Communist-run and to teach the Communist line. One of Goodbody's clients, having read that a certain Soviet economist had predicted the collapse of Western capitalism in 1946 and having noted that Western capitalism did, at the moment, show signs of collapsing, had concluded that the Communists must have the real lowdown on Wall Street, and decided to attend a session at the Jefferson School in the hope of getting some hot dope on the market. Gutman, though he was skeptical about the Party's talent for security analysis, and also a bit miffed that the customer should be attaching significance to any advice other than his, nevertheless allowed himself to be persuaded to go along. The two capitalists sat through an evening of earnest dialectic without picking up a single clue to the market's next move. When they finally left, the customer was snorting about a wasted evening, and Gutman was looking as smug as a cat.

It was in 1949 that Gutman was assigned to do the Goodbody weekly market letter, which he at first wrote in more or less conventional style. At about the same time, he took up art again, this time as a painter. He studied sketching, first with the sculptor Ben Karp and later with the abstract expressionist painter Jack Tworkov, and has since had two one-man shows of water colors and oils—at the Leonid Kipnis Gallery, in Westport, in 1954, and at the Poindexter Gallery, on West Fifty-sixth Street, in 1958. His styles of painting and market-letter writing evolved together, he has said, adding, by way of explanation, "I learned that each word had meanings radiating from it, the way space radiates from the lines in a drawing. I learned how to move words around in space, and thus get more interest." He moved words around in space so shrewdly that Goodbody & Company, in response to popular demand, gradually allowed the mailing list for his letter to expand from three thousand to twenty-two thousand. Meanwhile, Gutman was becoming moderately rich by following his own advice with his own money. He studied up on uranium, beryllium, lithium, boron, and other minerals used in the production of nuclear bombs and rocket fuels, and, through well-timed investments in mining companies, piled up profits that he found rather disconcerting. "I made so much money in the uranium boom that I got kind of ashamed of it," he says. Remorse has not led to abstinence, though; he admits to capital gains in the neighborhood of a quarter of a million dollars for a single recent year.

Much of Gutman's life today has been described by a friend of his as that of a sort of bee, busy at cultural cross-pollination. On the one hand, he constantly urges his Wall Street friends to buy modern paintings, including his own, and has tried—unsuccessfully, it is true—to persuade various promoters to have their stock certificates designed by the abstractionists Franz Kline and Willem de Kooning. On the other hand, he often beguiles his artistic and literary friends with dithyrambs on the stock market, and, to give these outbursts added punch, invests their money profitably for them.

Gutman's office at Shields & Company, where I visited him a while back, was a small, crowded room at the southeast corner of the twentieth floor of 44 Wall, where he sat facing his secretary at one of two cluttered desks, with an abstract painting by Mike Goldberg over his head, one by Kline on the wall opposite, a stock ticker at one elbow, and a typewriter at the other. Besides writing the weekly letter and making investments for himself, he got out a detailed research report on some company or other at least once a month, and handled the accounts of about fifty personal brokerage customers, most of whom gave him discretionary trading powers. His position at Shields was a rather anomalous one, because instead of being a member of the firm's regular research department, he constituted a separate, semi-independent section, set up expressly to attract individual investors through his letter. Since Shields & Company—whose name is probably best known to the general public through the yachting exploits of its partner and co-founder Cornelius Shields—was established, in 1923, it has engaged in brokerage, underwriting, and private deal-making; in the mid-thirties it had branch offices all over the country and was among the top five firms in volume of Stock Exchange business, but then, beginning in 1937, it concentrated more and more on underwriting and private deals, gradually contracting its brokerage business until by the end of 1957 it had no branch offices left except one in Buffalo and, as far as brokerage volume went, wasn't in a class with the ubiquitous multinominal giants of the commission trade. In the mid-fifties, the

Shields partners changed their minds and set out to recapture some of the lost brokerage business; the Buffalo office was enlarged, an office was opened in White Plains, a batch of hot new customers' men were rounded up, and Gutman was lured away from Goodbody. Whether it was the improved branch-office setup, the new customers' men, or the Gutman letter that did the trick, Shields's slice of Stock Exchange business shot up about 20 percent after Gutman came. He brought with him from Goodbody, as his assistant, a young security analyst named Walter Rizzuti, but Rizzuti made so much money on his own speculations during the second half of 1958 that he quit his job.

When Gutman isn't holed up in his cubby on Wall Street, he is likely to be out visiting some company—snooping around its laboratories and production lines, and pumping its officers for information. Like most practitioners of his trade, he considers such road trips very important, and he is generally thought to have a special talent for smoking out piquant tidbits of information from recalcitrant corporations. "Gutman asks questions in such a quiet, unassuming way that you tend to tell him more than you would a fellow who talks louder," says Joseph C. Abeles, president of the Kawecki Chemical Company, who has himself been taken off guard once or twice by Gutman's mild manner. Of course, most companies, being anxious to have their stocks go up, are only too glad to cooperate with security analysts, who may recommend the stocks to the public, but all conscientious company officers want to avoid giving special favors to any one analyst, and some old-line managements are just naturally close-mouthed. Gutman, however, is always hopeful of a scoop; on a personal visit, he feels, an indiscreet word may be dropped, or the door of a laboratory be left open, or the character of a top executive be unconsciously revealed. A few years ago, he went to Granite City, Illinois, to visit the Granite City Steel Company, a relatively small firm, about which he had grave misgivings, because he suspected its new president, John Marshall, of being a dabbler. Having been ushered into the president's office, he found Marshall seated not behind a desk but in an armchair adorned with a gay print slipcover—a circumstance that Gutman considered crushing evidence in support of his preconception. He asked Marshall a routine question about Granite City's plans for capital investment, and, as Gutman has since described the incident, "Marshall's thin hand waved elegantly with a lit cigarette in it—the way the hand of a rich man might wave at a cocktail party when he tells you he has bought another sports car—and he said, 'We're thinking of spending fifty to a hundred million.' " Gutman was so impressed by this revelation of foppishness masking decisiveness in the Scarlet Pimpernel tradition that he had what he calls a "moment of intuition," and subsequently gave Granite City a hearty recommendation. (Soon afterward, the company's stock bounded from 16 to 68.) On another occasion, he was visiting a large company that had just put a new miracle drug on the market. The expected sales of the drug were a carefully guarded secret, but an unwary laboratory guide let slip the production schedule for the next two years. Figuring out the anticipated sales total was then a simple matter, and Gutman had his scoop.

Professional opinions of Gutman as a security analyst range from the ecstatic to the cagey. At the ecstatic end is the late Raymond Trigger, a veteran Wall Street journalist who was managing editor of *Investment Dealers' Digest,* and who often watched Gutman at his snooping. "Walter knows his companies, especially his chemical companies, from A to Z," Trigger said. "He always has just the technical question that tells them he can't be bamboozled. Oh, God, he's good!" A few of his fellow analysts are so staggered by his literary gifts that they consider any comment on his economics niggling and irrelevant; at the Bankers Club one recent lunchtime, Sidney R. Winters, of Abraham & Company, plucked at Gutman's sleeve and told him, "Your last letter was wonderful. Never in my thirty-one years down here have I read anything that so poetically expressed such a deep fundamental philosophy." A less entranced fellow analyst, Michael S. Thomas, of R. W. Pressprich & Company, who specializes in finding sound investment opportunities for large institutions, thinks that while Gutman's work is often brilliant, it is seldom exhaustive enough for anyone who plans to plunge in more than a modest way. Pierre R. Bretey, of Hayden, Stone & Company, who is known in the Street as "the dean of railroad analysts" and as a pillar of conservative analytical thought, is even sterner in his judgment of Gutman, though still respectful. "His method of writing is not institutional," said Bretey, in 1959. "He's a modernist. Lately, he's been dealing in a heady brew of stocks in the rocket-and-missile fields, and it's been a very good market for him. What remains to be seen is whether he'll be nimble enough to call the turn when that group of stocks goes to hell in a hat. On balance, I'd say he's a good man, and he's made more money for his clients over the past couple of years than I've made for mine."

The Shields partners tended to treat Gutman like an exotic plant that must be handled with the utmost care, lest it stop blooming. "Walter's uniqueness is his ability to put his finger on the psychological effects of things as they relate to the stock market," one of them once told me, measuring his words. "Of course, what he writes isn't always exactly what I'd choose to have him write—and that's putting it mildly. But we want him to express himself without being hampered by editorship, provided it's always clear that the letter is his personal expression. What right have I to make him change things? Hell, can you tell a painter how to paint? Besides, he *does* stimulate brokerage business."

From Wall Street, Gutman often goes uptown to a spacious room over a bar-and-grill at 80 St. Marks Place, on the borderline between Greenwich Village and the lower East Side. This is where he does his painting. Most of his efforts up to now have been water color sketches of women, and practically all the remaining few have been oil or water color abstractions. One huge oil, some seven feet high and five wide, and entitled "Fire and Ice," is semiabstract; in it are the figures of two women, one dressed in brilliant yellows and reds and the other in dull greens and grays. Explaining it a while ago, Gutman said, with candor, "The composition came about rather casually. I was painting one model, you see, when another one, a friend of hers, walked into the studio, and the second girl looked so nice that I put her in, too. To the extent that the figures are abstract, they're that way not through intention but through incapacity. Still, it's a nice effect, don't you think?" Gutman is almost always modest about his work. "I'm only half serious about painting," he says. "I'm not trying to be Gauguin. After all, he quit finance and went to the South Seas, and I'm still in Wall Street." Nevertheless, Gutman's show at the Poindexter inspired the magazine *Art* to report that he showed a knack for "capturing in a few lines the litheness of figures," and to add, "Gutman has plainly been a serious artist for a number of years." His old instructor, Tworkov, says of Gutman, "He understands paint as few amateurs do. He truly reacts to painting—has a feeling for it, like an ear for music. He has great gusto and a limited amount of skill, like, say, an extremely primitive Matisse. Walter isn't very teachable, though. What he has is an ability to work without rules. To teach him more about painting would be to spoil the best thing he has. Incidentally, my opinion of Walter as a stock-market adviser is very lyrical."

As Gutman sees it, one of the greatest benefits he gets from being a painter is the opportunity, so often denied to businessmen and financiers, to associate easily with professional artists and writers. His creative friends regard him with affection, curiosity, and possibly a trace of economic lust, and it is plain that their image of his Wall Street world is considerably more romantic than his image of their literary and artistic one. "I'd say that Walter *is* an abstract painting," a young writer he knows remarked recently—somewhat obscurely, perhaps, but with feeling. Gutman frequently honors his literary acquaintances by submitting early drafts of his market letters to them for criticism, and some of them have become quite knowledgeable about stocks, at least in their own estimation. Sometimes the comment he gets is along the line of "Stylistically, I'd say it's a fine letter, but aren't you going a bit overboard on Foote Minerals?" Once his letter is printed, he sees to it that it is distributed to all the writers and painters he knows, whether they are investors or not. One such non-investing reader is Jack Kerouac. Encountering him at an art opening back in the heyday of Kerouac's fame as a beatnik hero, Gutman asked how he had liked the latest letter, which was on boron stocks. "I had a crazy dream the other night," Kerouac replied. "I dreamed boron was God." Gutman was so enchanted with this reaction that he based a subsequent letter on it. "Boron either is a sort of god, the way Kerouac dreamed, or it isn't," he wrote. "The people intimately concerned with the boron industry seem to think it is."

In 1959, Gutman achieved a wonderful synthesis of his life interests by entering into a business venture with Kerouac; Robert Frank, a photographer; and Alfred Leslie, a painter. The company produced short films, the first of which, entitled *Pull My Daisy,* was based on a play by Kerouac; in this, various poets, painters, and actors played the parts in pantomime while Kerouac intoned the speeches assigned to all of them. The film attained modest box-office returns but had a certain avant-garde vogue. The opening of the vital bank account for the new enterprise took place in the head office of the Manufacturers Trust Company, which is on the ground floor of 44 Wall. Present for the ceremony were Gutman, Frank, Leslie, and a Manufacturers Trust vice-president. (Kerouac was on the road at the time.) Gutman had been a little apprehensive about how his associates were going to look against a downtown background, and his uneasiness was not entirely unjustified; Frank, to be sure, appeared wearing a necktie and otherwise dressed in a style reasonably appropriate to the occasion, but Leslie, who has a longshoreman's physique and a ferocious expression that several years ago helped him win the title of "Mr. Bronx," showed up hatless and tieless, wearing an ancient, frayed shirt, and exhibiting the general attitude of a bull in a china shop. As things turned out, however, the ensuing half-hour conversation was singularly harmonious. At one point, the banker, after clearing his throat delicately, suggested that Leslie might give some account of his previous business experience. "Six months with Martha Jackson and six years with Tibor de Nagy," Leslie replied, referring to the two art galleries he has been associated with. This proved to be a far more telling reference than any of the partners had expected, because, although they weren't aware of it, Tibor de Nagy led a double life; when he wasn't managing the affairs of his art gallery, he was serving as a foreign representative in the home office of the Manufacturers Trust. It was just a matter of asking de Nagy to step across the hall, and Leslie was accorded not only a bank officer's voucher but also a resounding tribute as a most promising artist.

The rest of the session, except for a brief period on capitalization and the like, was devoted to a discussion of the best color for the new company's checks; the banker first suggested yellow, but Frank felt that something "more optimistic" was required, whereupon the banker brought out a sheaf of sample checks in all sorts of shades. Eventually, simple gray won out over salmon pink. Through the whole process, Gutman was beaming with the utmost satisfaction, and with good reason; clearly, it was a great day for cultural cross-pollination.

4 / A Corner in Piggly Wiggly

BETWEEN SPRING and midsummer, 1958, the common stock of the E. L. Bruce Company, the nation's leading maker of hardwood floors, moved from a low of just under $17 a share to a high of $190 a share. This startling, even alarming, rise was made in an ascending scale that was climaxed by a frantic crescendo in which the price went up a hundred dollars a share in a single day. Furthermore—and even more alarmingly—the rise did not seem to have the slightest bit of relation to any sudden hunger on the part of the American public for new hardwood floors. To the consternation of almost everyone concerned, conceivably including even some of the holders of Bruce stock, it seemed to be entirely the result of a technical stock-market situation called a corner. With the exception of a general panic such as occurred in 1929, a corner is the most drastic and spectacular of all developments that can occur in the stock market, and more than once in the nineteenth and early twentieth centuries, corners had threatened to wreck the national economy.

The Bruce situation never threatened to do that. For one thing, the Bruce Company was so small in relation to the economy as a whole that even the wildest gyrations in its stock could hardly have much national effect. For another, the Bruce "corner" was accidental—the by-product of a fight for corporate control—rather than the result of calculated manipulations, as most of the historic corners had been. Finally, this one eventually turned out to be not a true corner at all, but only a near thing; in September, Bruce stock quieted down and settled at a reasonable level. But the incident served to stir up memories, some of them perhaps tinged with nostalgia, among those flinty old Wall Streeters who had been around to see the classic corners—or at least the last of them.

In June of 1922, the New York Stock Exchange began listing the shares of a corporation called Piggly Wiggly Stores—a chain of retail self-service markets situated mostly in the South and West, with headquarters in Memphis—and the stage was set for one of the most dramatic financial battles of that gaudy decade when Wall Street, only negligently watched over by the federal government, was frequently sent reeling by the machinations of operators seeking to enrich themselves and destroy their enemies. Among the theatrical aspects of this particular battle—a battle so celebrated in its time that headline writers referred to it simply as the "Piggly Crisis"—was the personality of the hero (or, as some people saw it, the villain), who was a newcomer to Wall Street, a country boy setting out defiantly, amid the cheers of a good part of rural America, to lay the slick manipulators of New York by the heels. He was Clarence Saunders, of Memphis, a plump, neat, handsome man of forty-one who was already something of a legend in his home town, chiefly because of a house he was putting up there for himself. Called the Pink Palace, it was an enormous structure faced with pink Georgia marble and built around an awe-inspiring white-marble Roman atrium, and, according to Saunders, it would stand for a thousand years. Unfinished though it was, the Pink Palace was like nothing Memphis had ever seen before. Its grounds were to include a private golf course, since Saunders liked to do his golfing in seclusion. Even the makeshift estate where he and his wife and four children were camping out pending completion of the Palace had its own golf course. (Some people said that his preference for privacy was induced by the attitude of the local country club governors, who complained that he had corrupted their entire supply of caddies by the grandeur of his tips.) Saunders, who had founded the Piggly Wiggly Stores in 1919, had most of the standard traits of the flamboyant American promoter—suspect generosity, a knack for attracting publicity, love of ostentation, and so on—but he also had some much less common traits, notably a remarkably vivid style, both in speech and writing, and a gift, of which he may or may not have been aware, for comedy. But like so many great men before him, he had a weakness, a tragic flaw. It was that he insisted on thinking of himself as a hick, a boob, and a sucker, and, in doing so, he sometimes became all three.

This unlikely fellow was the man who engineered the last real corner in a nationally traded stock.

The game of Corner—for in its heyday it was a game, a high-stakes gambling game, pure and simple, embodying a good many of the characteristics of poker—was one phase of the endless Wall Street contest between bulls, who want the price of a stock to go up, and bears, who want it to go down. When a game of Corner was under way, the bulls' basic method of operation was, of course, to buy stock, and the bears' was to sell it. Since the average bear didn't own any of the stock issue in contest, he would resort to the common practice of selling short. When a short sale is made, the transaction is consummated with stock that the seller has borrowed (at a suitable rate of interest) from a broker. Since brokers are merely agents, and not outright owners, they, in turn, must borrow the stock themselves. This they do by tapping the "floating supply" of stock that is in constant circulation among investment houses—stock that private investors have left with one house or another for trading purposes, stock that is owned by estates and trusts and has been released for action under certain prescribed conditions, and so on. In essence, the floating supply consists of all the stock in a particular corporation that is available for trading and is not immured in a safe-deposit box or encased in a mattress. Though the supply floats, it is scrupulously kept track of; the short seller, borrowing, say, a thousand shares from his broker, knows that he has incurred an immutable debt. What he hopes—the hope that keeps him alive—is that the market price of the stock will go down, enabling him to buy the thousand shares he owes at a bargain rate, pay off his debt, and pocket the difference. What he risks is that the lender, for one reason or another, may demand that he deliver up his thousand borrowed shares at a moment when their market price is at a high. Then the grinding truth of the old Wall Street jingle is borne in upon him: "He who sells what isn't his'n must buy it back or go to prison." And in the days when corners were possible, the short seller's sleep was further disturbed by the fact that he was operating behind blank walls; dealing only with agents, he never knew either the identity of the purchaser of his stock (a prospective cornerer?) or the identity of the owner of the stock he had borrowed (the same prospective cornerer, attacking from the rear?).

Although it is sometimes condemned as being the tool of the speculator, short selling is still sanctioned, in a severely restricted form, on all of the nation's exchanges. In its unfettered state, it was the standard gambit in the game of Corner. The situation would be set up when a group of bears would go on a well-organized spree of short selling, and would often help their cause along by spreading rumors that the company back of the stock in question was on its last legs. This operation was called a bear raid. The bulls' most formidable—but, of course, riskiest—countermove was to try for a corner. As a rule, only a stock that many traders were selling short could be cornered; a stock that was in the throes of a real bear raid was ideal. In the latter situation, the would-be cornerer would attempt to buy up the investment houses' floating supply of the stock and enough of the privately held shares to freeze out the bears; if the attempt succeeded, when he called for the short sellers to make good the stock they had borrowed, they could buy it from no one but him. And they would have to buy it at any price he chose to ask, their only alternatives—at least theoretically—being to go into bankruptcy or to jail for failure to meet their obligations.

In the old days of titanic financial death struggles, when Adam Smith's ghost still smiled on Wall Street, corners were fairly common and were often extremely sanguinary, with hundreds of innocent bystanders, as well as the embattled principals, getting their financial heads lopped off. The most famous cornerer in history was that glorious old pirate, Commodore Cornelius Vanderbilt, who engineered no less than three successful corners during the eighteen-sixties. Probably his classic job was in the stock of the Harlem Railway. By dint of secretly buying up all its available shares while simultaneously circulating a series of scandalously untruthful rumors of imminent bankruptcy to lure the short sellers in, he achieved an airtight trap. Finally, with the air of a man doing them a favor by saving them from jail, he offered the cornered shorts at $179 a share the stock he had bought up at a small fraction of that figure. The most generally disastrous corner was that of 1901 in the stock of Northern Pacific; to raise the huge quantities of cash they needed to cover themselves, the Northern Pacific shorts sold so many other stocks as to cause a national panic with world-wide repercussions. The next-to-last great corner occurred in 1920, when Allan A. Ryan, in order to harass his enemies in the New York Stock Exchange, sought to corner the stock of the Stutz Motor Company, makers of the renowned Stutz Bearcat. Ryan achieved his corner and the Stock Exchange short sellers were duly squeezed. But Ryan, it turned out, had a bearcat by the tail. The Stock Exchange suspended Stutz dealings, lengthy litigation followed, and Ryan came out of the affair financially ruined.

Then, as at other times, the game of Corner suffered from a difficulty that plagues other games—post-mortem disputes about the rules. The reform legislation of the nineteen-thirties, by outlawing any short selling that is specifically intended to demoralize a stock, as well as other manipulations leading toward corners, virtually ruled the game out of existence. Wall Streeters who speak of the Corner these days are referring to the intersection of Broad and Wall. In U.S. stock markets, only an accidental corner (or near-corner, like the Bruce one) is now possible; Clarence Saunders was the last intentional player of the game.

Saunders has been variously characterized by people who knew him well as "a man of limitless imagination and energy," "arrogant and conceited as all getout," "essentially a four-year-old child, playing at things," and "one of the most remarkable men of his generation." But there is no doubt that even many of the people who lost money on his promotional schemes believed that he was the soul of honesty. He was born in 1881 to a poor family in Amherst County, Virginia, and in his teens was employed by the local grocer at the pittance that is orthodox for future tycoons taking on their first jobs—in his case, four dollars a week. Moving ahead fast, he went on to a wholesale grocery company in Clarksville, Tennessee, and then to one in Memphis, and, while still in his twenties, organized a small retail food chain called United Stores. He sold that after a few years, did a stint as a wholesale grocer on his own, and then, in 1919, began to build a chain of retail self-service markets, to which he gave the engaging name of Piggly Wiggly Stores. (When a Memphis business associate once asked him why he had chosen that name, he replied, "So people would ask me what you just did.") The stores flourished so exuberantly that by the autumn of 1922 there were over twelve hundred of them. Of these, some six hundred and fifty were owned outright by Saunders' Piggly Wiggly Stores, Inc.; the rest were independently owned, but their owners paid royalties to the parent company for the right to adopt its patented method of operations. In 1923, an era when a grocery store meant clerks in white aprons and often a thumb on the scale, this method was described by the *New York Times* with astonishment: "The customer in a Piggly Wiggly Store rambles down aisle after aisle, on both sides of which are shelves. The customer collects his purchases and pays as he goes out." Although Saunders did not know it, he had invented the supermarket.

A natural concomitant of the rapid rise of Piggly Wiggly Stores, Inc., was the acceptance of its shares for listing on the New York Stock Exchange, and within six months of that event Piggly Wiggly stock had become known as a dependable, if unsensational, dividend-payer—the kind of widows'-and-orphans' stock that speculators regard with the respectful indifference that crap-shooters feel about bridge. This reputation, however, was short-lived. In November, 1922, several small companies that had been operating grocery stores in New York, New Jersey, and Connecticut under the name Piggly Wiggly failed and went into receivership. These companies had scarcely any connection with Saunders' concern; he had merely sold them the right to use his firm's catchy trade name, leased them some patented equipment, and washed his hands of them. But when these independent Piggly Wigglys failed, a group of stock-market operators (whose identities never were revealed, because they dealt through tight-lipped brokers) saw in the situation a heaven-sent opportunity for a bear raid. If individual Piggly Wiggly stores were failing, they reasoned, then rumors could be spread that would lead the uninformed public to believe that the parent firm was failing, too. To further this belief, they began briskly selling Piggly Wiggly short, in order to force the price down. The stock yielded readily to their pressure, and within a few weeks its price, which earlier in the year had hovered around fifty dollars a share, dropped to below forty.

At this point, Saunders announced to the press that he was about to "beat the Wall Street professionals at their own game" with a buying campaign. He was by no means a professional himself; in fact, prior to the listing of Piggly Wiggly he had never owned a single share of any stock quoted on the New York Stock Exchange. There is little reason to believe that at the beginning of his buying campaign he had any intention of trying for a corner; it seems more likely that his announced motive—the unassailable one of supporting the price of the stock in order to protect his own investment and that of other Piggly Wiggly stockholders—was all he had in mind. In any case, he took on the bears with characteristic zest, supplementing his own funds with a loan of about ten million dollars from a group of bankers in Memphis, Nashville, New Orleans, Chattanooga, and St. Louis. Legend has it that he stuffed his ten million-plus, in bills of large denomination, into a suitcase, boarded a train for New York, and, his pockets bulging with currency that wouldn't fit in the suitcase, marched on Wall Street, ready to do battle. He emphatically denied this in later years, insisting that he had remained in Memphis and masterminded his campaign by means of telegrams and long-distance telephone calls to various Wall Street brokers. Wherever he was at the time, he did round up a corps of some twenty brokers, among them Jesse L. Livermore, who served as his chief of staff. Livermore, one of the most celebrated American speculators of this century, was then forty-five years old but was still occasionally, and derisively, referred to by the nickname he had earned a couple of decades earlier—the Boy Plunger of Wall Street. Since Saunders regarded Wall Streeters in general and speculators in particular as parasitic scoundrels intent only on battering down his stock, it seems likely that his decision to make an ally of Livermore was a reluctant one, arrived at simply with the idea of getting the enemy chieftain into his own camp.

On the first day of his duel with the bears, Saunders, operating behind his mask of brokers, bought 33,000 shares of Piggly Wiggly, mostly from the short sellers; within a week he had brought the total to 105,000—more than half of the 200,000 shares outstanding. Meanwhile, ventilating his emotions at the cost of tipping his hand, he began running a series of advertisements in which he vigorously and pungently told the readers of Southern and Western newspapers what he thought of Wall Street. "Shall the gambler rule?" he demanded in one of these effusions. "On a white horse he rides. Bluff is his coat of mail and thus shielded is a yellow heart. His helmet is deceit, his spurs clink with treachery, and the hoofbeats of his horse thunder destruction. Shall good business flee? Shall it tremble with fear? Shall it be the loot of the speculator?" On Wall Street, Livermore went on buying Piggly Wiggly.

The effectiveness of Saunders' buying campaign was readily apparent; by late January of 1923 it had driven the price of the stock up over 60, or higher than ever before. Then, to intensify the bear raiders' jitters, reports came in from Chicago, where the stock was also traded, that Piggly Wiggly was cornered—that the short sellers could not replace the stock they had borrowed without coming to Saunders for supplies. The reports were immediately denied by the New York Stock Exchange, which announced that the floating supply of Piggly Wiggly was ample, but they may have put an idea into Saunders' head, and this, in turn, may have prompted a curious and—at first glance—mystifying move he made in mid-February, when, in another widely disseminated newspaper advertisement, he offered to *sell* fifty thousand shares of Piggly Wiggly stock to the public at fifty-five dollars a share. The ad pointed out, persuasively enough, that the stock was paying a dividend of a dollar four times a year—a return of more than 7 percent. "This is to be a quick proposition, subject to withdrawal without prior notice," the ad went on, calmly but urgently. "To get in on the ground floor of any big proposition is the opportunity that comes to few, and then only once in a lifetime."

Anyone who is even slightly familiar with modern economic life can scarcely help wondering what the Securities and Exchange Commission, which is charged with seeing to it that all financial advertising is kept factual, impersonal, and unemotional, would have had to say about the hard sell in those last two sentences. But if Saunders' first stock-offering ad would have caused an S.E.C. examiner to turn pale, his second, published four days later, might well have induced an apoplectic seizure. A full-page affair, it cried out, in huge black type:

OPPORTUNITY! OPPORTUNITY!

> It Knocks! It Knocks! It Knocks!
> Do you hear? Do you listen? Do you understand?
> Do you wait? Do you act now? . . .
> Has a new Daniel appeared and the lions eat him not?
> Has a new Joseph come that riddles may be made plain?
> Has a new Moses been born to a new Promised Land?
> Why, then, asks the skeptical, can CLARENCE SAUNDERS . . . be so generous to the public?

After finally making it clear that he was selling common stock and not snake oil, Saunders repeated his offer to sell at fifty-five dollars a share, and went on to explain that he was being so generous because, as a farsighted businessman, he was anxious to have Piggly Wiggly owned by its customers and other small investors, rather than by Wall Street sharks. To many people, though, it appeared that Saunders was being generous to the point of folly. The price of Piggly Wiggly on the New York Stock Exchange was just then pushing 70; it looked as if Saunders were handing anyone who had fifty-five dollars in his pocket a chance to make fifteen dollars with no risk. The arrival of a new Daniel, Joseph, or Moses might be debatable, but opportunity certainly did seem to be knocking, all right.

Actually, as the skeptical must have suspected, there was a catch. In making what sounded like such a costly and unbusinesslike offer, Saunders, a rank novice at Corner, had devised one of the craftiest dodges ever used in the game. One of the great hazards in Corner was always that even though a player might defeat his opponents, he would discover that he had won a Pyrrhic victory. Once the short sellers had been squeezed dry, that is, the cornerer might find that the reams of stock he had accumulated in the process were a dead weight around his neck; by pushing it all back into the market in one shove, he would drive its price down close to zero. And if, like Saunders, he had had to borrow heavily to get into the game in the first place, his creditors could be expected to close in on him and perhaps not only divest him of his gains but drive him into bankruptcy. Saunders apparently anticipated this hazard almost as soon as a corner was in sight, and accordingly made plans to unload some of his stock before winning instead of afterward. His problem was to keep the stock he sold from going right back into the floating supply, thus breaking his corner; and his solution was to sell his fifty-five-dollar shares on the installment plan. In his February advertisements, he stipulated that the public could buy shares only by paying twenty-five dollars down and the balance in three ten-dollar installments, due June 1st, September 1st, and December 1st. In addition—and vastly more important—he said he would not turn over the stock certificates to the buyers until the final installment had been paid. Since the buyers obviously couldn't sell the certificates until they had them, the stock could not be used to replenish the floating supply. Thus Saunders had until December 1st to squeeze the short sellers dry.

Easy as it may be to see through Saunders' plan by hindsight, his maneuver was then so unorthodox that for a while neither the governors of the Stock Exchange nor Livermore himself could be quite sure what the man in Memphis was up to. The Stock Exchange began making formal inquiries, and Livermore began getting skittish, but he went on buying for Saunders' account, and succeeded in pushing Piggly Wiggly's price up well above 70. In Memphis, Saunders sat back comfortably; he temporarily ceased singing the praises of Piggly Wiggly stock in his ads, and devoted them to eulogizing apples, grapefruit, onions, hams, and Lady Baltimore cakes. Early in March, though, he ran another financial ad, repeating his stock offer and inviting any readers who wanted to discuss it with him to drop in at his Memphis office. He also emphasized that quick action was necessary; time was running out.

By now, it was apparent that Saunders was trying for a corner, and on Wall Street it was not only the Piggly Wiggly bears who were becoming apprehensive. Finally, Livermore, possibly reflecting that in 1908 he had lost almost a million dollars trying to get a corner in cotton, could stand it no longer. He demanded that Saunders come to New York and talk things over. Saunders arrived on the morning of March 12th. As he later described the meeting to reporters, there was a difference of opinion; Livermore, he said—and his tone was that of a man rather set up over having made a piker out of the Boy Plunger —"gave me the impression that he was a little afraid of my financial situation and that he did not care to be involved in any market crash." The upshot of the conference was that Livermore bowed out of the Piggly Wiggly operation, leaving Saunders to run it by himself. Saunders then boarded a train for Chicago to attend to some business there. At Albany, he was handed a telegram from a member of the Stock Exchange who was the nearest thing he had to a friend in the white-charger-and-coat-of-mail set. The telegram informed him that his antics had provoked a great deal of head-shaking in the councils of the Exchange, and urged him to stop creating a second market by advertising stock for sale at a price so far below the quotation on the Exchange. At the next station, Saunders telegraphed back a rather unresponsive reply. If it was a possible corner the Exchange was fretting about, he said, he could assure the governors that they could put their fears aside, since he himself was maintaining the floating supply by daily offering stock for loan in any amount desired. But he didn't say how long he would continue to do so.

A week later, on Monday, March 19th, Saunders ran a newspaper ad stating that his stock offer was about to be withdrawn; this was the last call. At the time, or so he claimed afterward, he had acquired all but 1,128 of Piggly Wiggly's 200,000 outstanding shares, for a total of 198,872, some of which he owned and the rest of which he "controlled"—a reference to the installment-plan shares whose certificates he still held. Actually, this figure was open to considerable argument (there was one private investor in Providence, for instance, who alone held eleven hundred shares), but there is no denying that Saunders had in his hands practically every single share of Piggly Wiggly then available for trading—and that he therefore had his corner. On that same Monday, it is believed, Saunders telephoned Livermore and asked if he would relent long enough to see the Piggly Wiggly project through by calling for delivery of all the shares that were owed Saunders; in other words, would Livermore please spring the trap? Nothing doing,

Livermore is supposed to have replied, evidently considering himself well out of the whole affair. So the following morning, Tuesday, March 20th, Saunders sprang the trap himself.

It turned out to be one of Wall Street's wilder days. Piggly Wiggly opened at 75½, up 5½ from the previous day's closing price. An hour after the opening, word arrived that Saunders had called for delivery of all his Piggly Wiggly stock. According to the rules of the Exchange, stock called for under such circumstances had to be produced by two-fifteen the following afternoon. But Piggly Wiggly, as Saunders well knew, simply wasn't to be had—except, of course, from him. To be sure, there were a few shares around that were still held by private investors, and frantic short sellers trying to shake them loose bid their price up and up. But by and large there wasn't much actual trading in Piggly Wiggly, because there was so little Piggly Wiggly to be traded. The Stock Exchange post where it was bought and sold became the center of a mob scene as two-thirds of the brokers on the floor clustered around it, a few of them to bid but most of them just to push, whoop, and otherwise get in on the excitement. Desperate short sellers bought Piggly Wiggly at 90, then at 100, then at 110. Reports of sensational profits made the rounds. The Providence investor, who had picked up his eleven hundred shares at 39 in the previous autumn, while the bear raid was in full cry, came to town to be in on the kill, unloaded his holdings at an average price of 105, and then caught an afternoon train back home, taking with him a profit of over seventy thousand dollars. As it happened, he could have done even better if he had bided his time; by noon, or a little after, the price of Piggly Wiggly had risen to 124, and it seemed destined to zoom straight through the lofty roof above the traders' heads. But 124 was as high as it went, for that figure had barely been recorded when a rumor reached the floor that the governors of the Exchange were meeting to consider the suspension of further trading in the stock and the postponement of the short sellers' deadline for delivery. The effect of such action would be to give the bears time to beat the bushes for stock, and thus to weaken, if not break, Saunders' corner. On the basis of the rumor alone, Piggly Wiggly fell to 82 by the time the Exchange's closing bell ended the chaotic session.

The rumor proved to be true. After the close of business, the Governing Committee of the Exchange announced both the suspension of trading in Piggly Wiggly and the extension of the short sellers' delivery deadline "until further action by this committee." There was no immediate official reason given for this decision, but some members of the committee unofficially let it be known that they had been afraid of a repetition of the Northern Pacific panic if the corner were not broken. On the other hand, irreverent sideliners were inclined to wonder whether the Governing Committee had not been moved by the pitiful plight of the cornered short sellers, many of whom—as in the Stutz Motor case two years earlier—were believed to be members of the Exchange.

Despite all this, Saunders, in Memphis, was in a jubilant, expansive mood that Tuesday evening. After all, his paper profits at that moment ran to several million dollars. The hitch, of course, was that he could not realize them, but he seems to have been slow to grasp that fact or to understand the extent to which his position had been undermined. The indications are that he went to bed convinced that, besides having personally brought about a first-class mess on the hated Stock Exchange, he had made himself a bundle and had demonstrated how a poor Southern boy could teach the city slickers a lesson. It all must have added up to a heady sensation. But, like most such sensations, it didn't last long. By Wednesday evening, when Saunders issued his first public utterance on the Piggly Crisis, his mood had changed to an odd mixture of puzzlement, defiance, and a somewhat muted echo of the crow-ing triumph of the night before. "A razor to my throat, figuratively speaking, is why I suddenly and without warning kicked the pegs from under Wall Street and its gang of gamblers and market manipulators," he declared in a press interview. "It was strictly a question of whether I should survive, and likewise my business and the fortunes of my friends, or whether I should be 'licked' and pointed to as a boob from Tennessee. And the consequence was that the boastful and supposedly invulnerable Wall Street powers found their methods controverted by well-laid plans and quick action." Saunders wound up his statement by laying down his terms: the Stock Exchange's deadline extension notwithstanding, he would expect settlement in full on all short stock by 3 P.M. the next day—Thursday—at $150 a share; thereafter his price would be $250.

On Thursday, to Saunders' surprise, very few short sellers came forward to settle; presumably those who did couldn't stand the uncertainty. But then the Governing Committee kicked the pegs from under Saunders by announcing that the stock of Piggly Wiggly was permanently stricken from its trading list and that the short sellers would be given a full five days from the original deadline—that is, until two-fifteen the following Monday—to meet their obligations. In Memphis, Saunders, far removed from the scene though he was, could not miss the import of these moves—he was now on the losing end of things. Nor could he any longer fail to see that the postponement of the short sellers' deadline was the vital issue. "As I understand it," he said in another statement, handed to reporters that evening, "the failure of a broker to meet his clearings through the Stock Exchange at the appointed time is the same as a bank that would be unable to meet its clearings, and all of us know what would happen to that kind of a bank. . . . The bank examiner would have a sign stuck up on the door with the word 'Closed.' It is unbelievable to me that the august and all-powerful New York Stock Exchange is a welcher. Therefore I continue to believe that the . . . shares of stock still due me on contracts . . . will be settled on the proper basis." An editorial in the Memphis *Commercial Appeal* backed up Saunders' cry of treachery, declaring, "This looks like what gamblers call welching. We hope the home boy beats them to a frazzle."

That same Thursday, by a coincidence, the annual financial report of Piggly Wiggly Stores, Inc., was made public. It was a highly favorable one—sales, profits, current assets, and all other significant figures were up sharply over the year before—but nobody paid any attention to it. For the moment, the real worth of the company was irrelevant; the point was the game.

On Friday morning, the Piggly Wiggly bubble burst. It burst because Saunders, who had said his price would rise to $250 a share after 3 P.M. Thursday, made the startling announcement that he would settle for a hundred. E. W. Bradford, Saunders' New York lawyer, was asked why Saunders had suddenly granted this striking concession. Saunders had done it out of the generosity of his heart, Bradford replied gamely, but the truth was soon obvious: Saunders had made the concession because he'd had to. The postponement granted by the Stock Exchange had given the short sellers and their brokers a chance to scan lists of Piggly Wiggly stockholders, and from these they had been able to smoke out small blocks of shares that Saunders had not cornered. Widows and orphans in Albuquerque and Sioux City, who knew nothing about short sellers and corners, were only too happy, when pressed, to dig into their mattresses or safe-deposit boxes and sell—in the so-called over-the-counter market, since the stock could no longer be traded on the Exchange—their ten or twenty shares of Piggly Wiggly for at least double what they had paid for them. Consequently, instead of having to buy stock from Saunders at his price of $250 and then hand it back to him in settlement of their loans, many of the short sellers were able to buy it in over-the-counter trading at around a hundred dollars, and thus, with bitter pleasure, pay off their Memphis adversary not in cash but in shares of Piggly Wiggly—the very last thing he wanted just then. By nightfall Friday, virtually all the short sellers were in the clear, having redeemed their indebtedness either by these over-the-counter purchases or by paying Saunders cash at his own suddenly deflated rate of a hundred dollars a share.

That evening, Saunders released still another statement, and this one, while still defiant, was unmistakably a howl of anguish. "Wall Street got licked and then called for 'mamma,'" it read. "Of all the institutions in America, the New York Stock Exchange is the worst menace of all in its power to ruin all who dare to oppose it. A law unto itself . . . an association of men who claim the right that no king or autocrat ever dared to take: to make a rule that applies one day on contracts and abrogate it the next day to let out a bunch of welchers. . . . My whole life from this day on will be aimed toward the end of having the public protected from a like occurrence. . . . I am not afraid. Let Wall Street get me if they can." But it appeared that Wall Street had got him; his corner was broken, leaving him deeply in debt to the syndicate of Southern bankers and encumbered with a mountain of stock whose immediate future was, to say the least, precarious.

Saunders' fulminations did not go unheeded on Wall Street, and as a result the Exchange felt compelled to justify itself. On Monday, March 26th, shortly after the Piggly Wiggly short sellers' deadline had passed and Saunders' corner was, for all practical purposes, a dead issue, the Exchange offered its apologia, in the form of a lengthy review of the crisis from beginning to end. In presenting its case, the Exchange emphasized the public harm that might have been done if the corner had gone unbroken, explaining, "The enforcement simultaneously of all contracts for the return of the stock would have forced the stock to any price that might be fixed by Mr. Saunders, and competitive bidding for the insufficient supply might have brought about conditions illustrated by other corners, notably the Northern Pacific corner in 1901." Then, its syntax yielding to its sincerity, the Exchange went on to say that "the demoralizing effects of such a situation are not limited to those directly affected by the contracts but extends to the whole market." Getting down to the two specific actions it had taken—the suspension of trading in Piggly Wiggly and the extension of the short sellers' deadline—the Exchange argued that both of them were within the bounds of its own constitution and rules, and therefore irreproachable. Arrogant as this may sound now, the Exchange had a point; in those days its rules were just about the only controls over stock trading.

The question of whether, even by their own rules, the slickers really played fair with the boob is still being debated among fiscal antiquarians. There is strong presumptive evidence that the slickers themselves later came to have their doubts. Regarding the right of the Exchange to suspend trading in a stock there can be no argument, since the right was, as the Exchange claimed at the time, specifically granted in its constitution. But the right to postpone the deadline for short sellers to honor their contracts, though also claimed at the time, is another matter. In June, 1925, two years after Saunders' corner, the Exchange felt constrained to amend its constitution with an article stating that "whenever in the opinion of the Governing Committee a corner has been created in a security listed on the Exchange . . . the Governing Committee may postpone the time for deliveries on Exchange contracts therein." By adopting a statute authorizing it to do what it had done long before, the Exchange would seem, at the very least, to have exposed a guilty conscience.

The immediate aftermath of the Piggly Crisis was a wave of sympathy for Saunders. Throughout the hinterland, the public image of him became that of a gallant champion of the underdog who had been ruthlessly crushed. Even in New York, the very lair of the Stock Exchange, the *Times* conceded in an editorial that in the minds of many people Saunders represented St. George and the Stock Exchange the dragon. That the dragon triumphed in the end, said the *Times,* was "bad news for a nation at least 66⅔ per cent 'sucker,' which had its moment of triumph when it read that a sucker had trimmed the interests and had his foot on Wall Street's neck while the vicious manipulators gasped their lives away."

Not a man to ignore such a host of friendly fellow suckers, Saunders went to work to turn them to account. And he needed them, for his position was perilous indeed. His biggest problem was what to do about the ten million dollars that he owed his banker backers—and didn't have. The basic plan behind his corner—if he had had any plan at all—must have been to make such a killing that he could pay back a big slice of his debt out of the profits, pay back the rest out of the proceeds from his public stock sale, and then walk off with a still huge block of Piggly Wiggly stock free and clear. Even though the cut-rate hundred-dollar settlement had netted him a killing by most men's standards (just how much of a killing is not known, but it has been reliably estimated at half a million or so), it was not a fraction of what he might have reasonably expected it to be, and because it wasn't his whole structure became an arch without a keystone.

Having paid his bankers what he had received from the short sellers and from his public stock sale, Saunders found that he still owed them about five million dollars, half of it due September 1, 1923, and the balance on January 1, 1924. His best hope of raising the money lay in selling more of the vast bundle of Piggly Wiggly shares he still had on hand. Since he could no longer sell them on the Exchange, he resorted to his favorite form of self-expression—newspaper advertising, this time supplemented with a mail-order pitch offering Piggly

Wiggly again at fifty-five dollars. It soon became evident, though, that public sympathy was one thing and public willingness to translate sympathy into cash was quite another. Everyone, whether in New York, Memphis, or Texarkana, knew about the recent speculative shenanigans in Piggly Wiggly and about the dubious state of the president's finances. Not even Saunders' fellow suckers would have any part of his deal now, and the campaign was a bleak failure.

Sadly accepting this fact, Saunders next appealed to the local and regional pride of his Memphis neighbors by turning his remarkable powers of persuasion to the job of convincing them that his financial dilemma was a civic issue. If he should go broke, he argued, it would reflect not only on the character and business acumen of Memphis but on Southern honor in general. "I do not ask for charity," he wrote in one of the large ads he always seemed able to find the cash for, "and I do not request any flowers for my financial funeral, but I do ask . . . everybody in Memphis to recognize and know that this is a serious statement made for the purpose of acquainting those who wish to assist in this matter, that they may work with me, and with other friends and believers in my business, in a Memphis campaign to have every man and woman who possibly can in this city become one of the partners of the Piggly Wiggly business, because it is a good investment first, and, second, because it is the right thing to do." Raising his sights in a second ad, he declared, "For Piggly Wiggly to be ruined would shame the whole South."

Just which argument proved the clincher in persuading Memphis that it should try to pull Saunders' chestnuts out of the fire is hard to say, but some part of his line of reasoning clicked, and soon the Memphis *Commercial Appeal* was urging the town to get behind the embattled local boy. The response of the city's business leaders was truly inspiring to Saunders. A whirlwind three-day campaign was planned, with the object of selling fifty thousand shares of his stock to the citizens of Memphis at the old magic figure of fifty-five dollars a share; in order to give buyers some degree of assurance that they would not later find themselves alone out on a limb, it was stipulated that unless the whole block was sold within the three days, all sales would be called off. The Chamber of Commerce sponsored the drive; the American Legion, the Civitan Club, and the Exchange Club fell into line; and even the Bowers Stores and the Arrow Stores, both competitors of Piggly Wiggly in Memphis, agreed to plug the worthy cause. Hundreds of civic-minded volunteers signed up to ring doorbells. On May 3rd, five days before the scheduled start of the campaign, 250 Memphis businessmen assembled at the Gayoso Hotel for a kickoff dinner. There were cheers when Saunders, accompanied by his wife, entered the dining room; one of the many after-dinner speakers described him as "the man who has done more for Memphis than any in the last thousand years"—a rousing tribute that put God knew how many Chickasaw chiefs in their place. "Business rivalries and personal differences were swept away like mists before the sun," a *Commercial Appeal* reporter wrote of the dinner.

The drive got off to a splendid start. On the opening day—May 8th—society women and Boy Scouts paraded the streets of Memphis wearing badges that read, "We're One Hundred Per Cent for Clarence Saunders and Piggly Wiggly." Merchants adorned their windows with placards bearing the slogan "A Share of Piggly Wiggly Stock in Every Home." Telephones and doorbells rang incessantly. In short order, 23,698 of the 50,000 shares had been subscribed for. Yet at the very moment when most of Memphis had become miraculously convinced that the peddling of Piggly Wiggly stock was an activity fully as uplifting as soliciting for the Red Cross or the Community Chest, ugly doubts were brewing, and some vipers in the home nest suddenly demanded that Saunders consent to an immediate spot audit of his company's books. Saunders, for whatever reasons, refused, but offered to placate the skeptics by stepping down as president of Piggly Wiggly if such a move "would facilitate the stock-selling campaign." He was not asked to give up the presidency, but on May 9th, the second day of the campaign, a watchdog committee of four—three bankers and a businessman—was appointed by the Piggly Wiggly directors to help him run the company for an interim period, while the dust settled. That same day, Saunders was confronted with another embarrassing situation: why, the campaign leaders wanted to know, was he continuing to build his million-dollar Pink Palace at a time when the whole town was working for him for nothing? He replied hastily that he would have the place boarded up the very next day and that there would be no further construction until his financial future looked bright again.

The confusion attendant on these two issues brought the drive to a standstill. At the end of the third day, the total number of shares subscribed for was still under 25,000, and the sales that had been made were canceled. Saunders had to admit that the drive had been a failure. "Memphis has fizzled," he reportedly added—although he was at great pains to deny this a few years later, when he needed more of Memphis' money for a new venture. It would not be surprising, though, if he had made some such imprudent remark, for he was understandably suffering from a case of frazzled nerves, and was showing the strain. Just before the announcement of the campaign's unhappy end, he went into a closed conference with several Memphis business leaders and came out of it with a bruised cheekbone and a torn collar. None of the other men at the meeting showed any marks of violence. It just wasn't Saunders' day.

Although it was never established that Saunders had had his hand improperly in the Piggly Wiggly corporate till during his cornering operation, his first business move after the collapse of his attempt to unload stock suggested that he had at least had good reason to refuse a spot audit of the company's books. In spite of futile grunts of protest from the watchdog committee, he began selling not Piggly Wiggly stock but Piggly Wiggly stores—partly liquidating the company, that is—and no one knew where he would stop. The Chicago stores went first, and those in Denver and Kansas City soon followed. His announced intention was to build up the company's treasury so that *it* could buy the stock that the public had spurned, but there was some suspicion that the treasury desperately needed a transfusion just then —and not of Piggly Wiggly stock, either. "I've got Wall Street and the whole gang licked," Saunders reported cheerfully in June. But in mid-August, with the September 1st deadline for repayment of two and a half million dollars on his loan staring him in the face and with nothing like that amount of cash either on hand or in prospect, he resigned as president of Piggly Wiggly Stores, Inc., and turned over his assets—his stock in the company, his Pink Palace, and all the rest of his property—to his creditors.

It remained only for the formal stamp of failure to be put on Saunders personally and on Piggly Wiggly under his management. On August 22nd, the New York auction firm of Adrian H. Muller & Son, which dealt in so many next-to-worthless stocks that its salesroom was often called "the securities graveyard," knocked down fifteen hundred shares of Piggly Wiggly at a dollar a share—the traditional price for securities that have been run into the ground—and the following spring Saunders went through formal bankruptcy proceedings. But these were anticlimaxes. The real low point of Saunders' career was probably the day he was forced out of his company's presidency, and it was then that, in the opinion of many of his admirers, he achieved his rhetorical peak. When he emerged, harassed but still defiant, from a directors' conference and announced his resignation to reporters, a hush fell. Then Saunders added hoarsely, "They have the body of Piggly Wiggly, but they cannot have the soul."

If by the soul of Piggly Wiggly Saunders meant himself, then it did remain free—free to go marching on in its own erratic way. He never ventured to play another game of Corner, but his spirit was far from broken. Although officially bankrupt, he managed to find people of truly rocklike faith who were still willing to finance him, and they enabled him to live on a scale only slightly less grand than in the past; reduced to playing golf at the Memphis Country Club rather than on his own private course, he handed out caddy tips that the club governors considered as corrupting as ever. To be sure, he no longer owned the Pink Palace, but this was about the only evidence that served to remind his fellow townsmen of his misfortunes. Eventually, the unfinished pleasure dome came into the hands of the city of Memphis, which appropriated $150,000 to finish it and turn it into a museum of natural history and industrial arts. As such, it continues to sustain the Saunders legend in Memphis.

After his downfall, Saunders spent the better part of three years in seeking redress of the wrongs that he felt he had suffered in the Piggly Wiggly fight, and in foiling the efforts of his enemies and creditors to make things still more unpleasant for him. For a while, he kept threatening to sue the Stock Exchange for conspiracy and breach of contract, but a test suit, brought by some small Piggly Wiggly stockholders, failed, and he dropped the idea. Then, in January, 1926, he learned that a federal indictment was about to be brought against him for using the mails to defraud in his mail-order campaign to sell his Piggly Wiggly stock. He believed, incorrectly, that the government had been egged on to bring the indictment by an old associate of his—John C. Burch, of Memphis, who had become secretary-treasurer of Piggly Wiggly after the shakeup. His patience once more exhausted, Saunders went around to Piggly Wiggly headquarters and confronted Burch. This conference proved far more satisfactory to Saunders than his board-room scuffle on the day the Memphis civic stock-selling drive failed. Burch, according to Saunders, "undertook in a stammering way to deny" the accusation, whereupon Saunders delivered a right to the jaw, knocking off Burch's glasses but not doing much other damage. Burch afterward belittled the blow as "glancing," and added an alibi that sounded like that of any outpointed pugilist: "The assault upon me was made so suddenly that I did not have time or opportunity to strike Mr. Saunders." Burch refused to press charges.

About a month later, the mail-fraud indictment was brought against Saunders, but by that time, satisfied that Burch was innocent of any dirty work, he was his amiable old self again. "I have only one thing to regret in this new affair," he announced pleasantly, "and that is my fistic encounter with John C. Burch." The new affair didn't last long; in April the indictment was quashed by the Memphis District Court, and Saunders and Piggly Wiggly were finally quits. By then, the company was well on its way back up, and, with a greatly changed corporate structure, it flourishes to this day; housewives still ramble down the aisles of hundreds of Piggly Wiggly stores, which are now operated under a franchise agreement with the Piggly Wiggly Corporation, of Jacksonville, Florida.

Saunders, too, was well on his way back up. In 1928, he started a new grocery chain, which he—but hardly anyone else—called the Clarence Saunders, Sole Owner of My Name, Stores, Inc. Its outlets soon came to be known as Sole Owner stores, which was precisely what they weren't, for without Saunders' faithful backers they would have existed only in his mind. Saunders' choice of a corporate title, however, was not designed to mislead the public; rather, it was his ironic way of reminding the world that, after the skinning Wall Street had given him, his name was about the only thing he still had a clear title to. How many Sole Owner customers—or governors of the Stock Exchange, for that matter—got the point is questionable. In any case, the new stores caught on so rapidly and did so well that Saunders leaped back up from bankruptcy to riches, and bought a million-dollar estate just outside Memphis. He also organized and underwrote a professional football team called the Sole Owner Tigers—an investment that paid off handsomely on the fall afternoons when he could hear cries of "Rah! Rah! Rah! Sole Owner! Sole Owner! Sole Owner!" ringing through the Memphis Stadium.

For the second time, Saunders' glory was fleeting. The very first wave of the depression hit Sole Owner Stores such a crushing blow that in 1930 they went bankrupt, and he was broke again. But again he pulled himself together and survived the debacle. Finding backers, he planned a new chain of grocery stores, and thought up a name for it that was more outlandish, if possible, than either of its predecessors —Keedoozle. He never made another killing, however, or bought another million-dollar estate, though it was always clear that he expected to. His hopes were pinned on the Keedoozle, an electrically operated grocery store, and he spent the better part of the last twenty years of his life trying to perfect it. In a Keedoozle store, the merchandise was displayed behind glass panels, each with a slot beside it, like the food in an Automat. There the similarity ended, for, instead of inserting coins in the slot to open a panel and lift out a purchase, Keedoozle customers inserted a key that they were given on entering the store. Moreover, Saunders' thinking had advanced far beyond the elementary stage of having the key open the panel; each time a Keedoozle key was inserted in a slot, the identity of the item selected was inscribed in code on a segment of recording tape embedded in the key itself, and simultaneously the item was automatically transferred to a conveyor belt that carried it to an exit gate at the front of the store. When a customer had finished his shopping, he would present his key to an attendant at the gate, who would decipher the tape and add up the bill. As soon as this was paid, the purchases would be catapulted into the customer's arms, all bagged and wrapped, by a device at the end of the conveyor belt.

A couple of pilot Keedoozle stores were tried out—one in Memphis and the other in Chicago—but it was found that the machinery was too complex and expensive to compete with supermarket pushcarts. Undeterred, Saunders set to work on an even more intricate mechanism—the Foodelectric, which would do everything the Keedoozle could do and add up the bill as well. It will never corner the retail-store-equipment market, though, because it was still unfinished when Saunders died, in October, 1953. For better or worse, American finance will not soon look upon his like again.

5 / The Impacted Philosophers

AMONG THE GREATEST problems facing American industry today, one may learn by talking with any of a large number of industrialists who are not known to be especially given to pontificating, is "the problem of communication." This preoccupation with the difficulty of getting a thought out of one head and into another is something the industrialists share with a substantial number of intellectuals and creative writers, more and more of whom seem inclined to regard communication, or the lack of it, as one of the greatest problems not just of industry but of humanity. (A few avant-garde writers and artists have given the importance of communication a backhanded boost by flatly and unequivocally proclaiming themselves to be *against* it.) As far as the industrialists are concerned, I admit that in the course of hearing them invoke the word "communication"—often in an almost mystical way—over the past few years I have had a lot of trouble figuring out exactly what they meant. The general thesis is clear enough; namely, that everything would be all right, first, if they could get through to each other within their own organizations, and, second, if they, or their organizations, could get through to everybody else. What has puzzled me is how and why, in this day when the foundations sponsor one study of communication after another, individuals and organizations fail so consistently to express themselves understandably, or how and why their listeners fail to grasp what they hear.

Recently, I acquired a two-volume publication of the United States Government Printing Office entitled *Hearings Before the Subcommittee on Antitrust and Monopoly of the Committee on the Judiciary, United States Senate, Eighty-seventh Congress, First Session, Pursuant to S. Res. 52,* and after a fairly diligent perusal of its 1,459 pages I think I begin to see what the industrialists are talking about. The hearings, conducted in April, May, and June, 1961, under the chairmanship of Senator Estes Kefauver, of Tennessee, had to do with the now famous price-fixing and bid-rigging conspiracies in the electrical-manufacturing industry, which had already resulted, the previous February, in the imposition by a federal judge in Philadelphia of fines totaling $1,924,-500 on twenty-nine firms and forty-five of their employees, and also of thirty-day prison sentences on seven of the employees. Since there had been no public presentation of evidence, all the defendants having pleaded either guilty or no defense, and since the records of the grand juries that indicted them were secret, the public had had little opportunity to hear about the details of the violations, and Senator Kefauver felt that the whole matter needed a good airing. The transcript shows that it got one, and what the airing revealed—at least within the biggest company involved—was a breakdown in intramural communication so drastic as to make the building of the Tower of Babel seem a triumph of organizational rapport.

In a series of indictments brought by the government in the United States District Court in Philadelphia between February and October, 1960, the twenty-nine companies and their executives were charged with having repeatedly violated Section 1 of the Sherman Act of 1890, which declares illegal "every contract, combination in the form of trust or otherwise, or conspiracy, in restraint of trade or commerce among the several States, or with foreign nations." (The Sherman Act was the instrument used in the celebrated trust-busting activities of Theodore Roosevelt, and along with the Clayton Act of 1914 it has served as the government's weapon against cartels and monopolies ever since.) The violations, the government alleged, were committed in connection with the sale of large and expensive pieces of apparatus of a variety that is required chiefly by public and private electric-utility companies (power transformers, switchgear assemblies, and turbine-generator units, among many others), and were the outcome of a series of meetings attended by executives of the supposedly competing companies—beginning at least as early as 1956 and continuing into 1959—at which noncompetitive price levels were agreed upon, nominally sealed bids on individual contracts were rigged in advance, and each company was allocated a certain percentage of the available business. The government further alleged that, in an effort to preserve the secrecy of these meetings, the executives had resorted to such devices as referring to their companies by code numbers in their correspondence, making telephone calls from public booths or from their homes rather than from their offices, and doctoring the expense accounts covering their get-togethers to conceal the fact that they had all been in a certain city on a certain day. But their stratagems did not prevail. The federals, forcefully led by Robert A. Bicks, then head of the Antitrust Division of the Department of Justice, succeeded in exposing them, with considerable help from some of the conspirators themselves, who, after an employee of a small conspirator company saw fit to spill the beans in the early fall of 1959, flocked to turn state's evidence.

The economic and social significance of the whole affair may be demonstrated clearly enough by citing just a few figures. In an average year, a total of more than one and three-quarters billion dollars is spent to purchase machines of the sort in question, nearly a fourth of it by federal, state, and local governments (which, of course, means the taxpayers), and most of the rest by private utility companies (which are inclined to pass along any rise in the cost of their equipment to the public in the form of rate increases). To take a specific example of the kind of money involved in an individual transaction, the list price of a 500,000-kilowatt turbine-generator—a monstrous device for producing electric power from steam power—may be something like sixteen million dollars. Actually, manufacturers have sometimes cut their prices by as much as 25 percent in order to make a sale, and therefore, if everything is aboveboard, it may be possible to buy the machine at a saving of four million dollars; if representatives of the companies making such generators hold a single meeting and agree to fix prices, they may, in effect, increase the cost to the customer by the four million. And in the end, the customer is almost sure to be the public.

In presenting the indictments in Philadelphia, Bicks stated that, considered collectively, they revealed "a pattern of violations which can fairly be said to range among the most serious, the most flagrant, the most pervasive that have ever marked any basic American industry." Just before imposing the sentences, Judge J. Cullen Ganey went even further; in his view, the violations constituted "a shocking indictment of a vast section of our economy, for what is really at stake here is the survival of . . . the free-enterprise system." The prison sentences showed that he meant it; although there had been many successful prosecutions for violation of the Sherman Act during the seven decades since its passage, it was rare indeed for executives to be jailed. Not surprisingly, therefore, the case kicked up quite a ruckus in the press. The *New Republic,* to be sure, complained that the newspapers and magazines were intentionally playing down "the biggest business scandal in decades," but the charge did not seem to have much foundation. Considering such things as the public's apathy toward switchgear, the woeful bloodlessness of criminal cases involving antitrust laws, and the relatively few details of the conspiracies that had emerged, the press in general gave the story a good deal of space, and even the *Wall Street Journal* and *Fortune* ran uncompromising and highly informative accounts of the debacle; here and there, in fact, one could detect signs of a revival of the spirit of old-time antibusiness journalism as it existed back in the thirties. After all, what could be more exhilarating than to see several dignified, impeccably tailored, and highly paid executives of a few of the nation's most respected corporations being trooped off to jail like common pickpockets? It was certainly the biggest moment for business-baiters since 1938, when Richard Whitney, the president of the New York Stock Exchange at the time, was put behind bars for speculating with his customers' money. Some called it the biggest since Teapot Dome.

To top it all off, there was a prevalent suspicion of hypocrisy in the very highest places. Neither the chairman of the board nor the president of General Electric, the largest of the corporate defendants, had been caught in the government's dragnet, and the same was true of Westinghouse Electric, the second-largest; these four ultimate bosses let it be known that they had been entirely ignorant of what had been going on within their commands right up to the time the first testimony on the subject was given to the Justice Department. Many people, however, were not satisfied by these disclaimers, and, instead, took the position that the defendant executives were men in the middle, who had broken the law only in response either to actual orders or to a corporate climate favoring price-fixing, and who were now being allowed to suffer for the sins of their superiors. Among the unsatisfied was Judge Ganey himself, who said at the time of the sentencing, "One would be most naïve indeed to believe that these violations of the law, so long persisted in, affecting so large a segment of the industry, and, finally, involving so many millions upon millions of dollars, were facts unknown to those responsible for the conduct of the corporation. . . . I am convinced that in the great number of these defendants' cases, they were torn between conscience and approved corporate policy, with the rewarding objectives of promotion, comfortable security, and large salaries."

The public naturally wanted a ringleader, an archconspirator, and it appeared to find what it wanted in General Electric, which—to the acute consternation of the men endeavoring to guide its destinies from company headquarters, at 570 Lexington Avenue, New York City—got the lion's share of attention both in the press and in the Subcommittee hearings. With some 300,000 employees, and sales averaging some four billion dollars a year over the past ten years, it was not only far and away the biggest of the twenty-nine accused companies but, judged on the basis of sales in 1959, the fifth-biggest company in the country. It also drew a higher total of fines ($437,500) than any other company, and saw more of its executives sent to jail (three, with eight others receiving suspended sentences). Furthermore, as if to intensify in this hour of crisis the horror and shock of true believers—and the glee of scoffers—its highest-ranking executives had for years tried to represent it to the public as a paragon of successful virtue by issuing encomiums to the free competitive system, the very system that the price-fixing meetings were set up to mock. In 1959, shortly after the government's investigation of the violations had been brought to the attention of G.E.'s policymakers, the company demoted and cut the pay of those of its executives who admitted that they had been involved; one vice-president, for example, was informed that instead of the $127,000 a year he had been getting he would now get $40,000. (He had scarcely adjusted himself to that blow when Judge Ganey fined him four thousand dollars and sent him to prison for thirty days, and shortly after he regained his freedom, General Electric eased him out entirely.) The G.E. policy of imposing penalties of its own on these employees, regardless of what punishment the court might prescribe, was not adopted by Westinghouse, which waited until the judge had disposed of the case and then decided that the fines and prison sentences he had handed out to its stable of offenders were chastisement enough, and did not itself penalize them at all. Some people saw this attitude as evidence that Westinghouse was condoning the conspiracies, but others regarded it as a commendable, if tacit, admission that management at the highest level in the conniving companies was responsible—morally, at least—for the whole mess and was therefore in no position to discipline its erring employees. In the view of these people, G.E.'s haste to penalize the acknowledged culprits on its payroll strongly suggested that the firm was trying to save its own skin by throwing a few luckless employees to the wolves, or—as Senator Philip A. Hart, of Michigan, put it, more pungently, during the hearings—"to do a Pontius Pilate operation."

Embattled days at 570 Lexington Avenue! After years of cloaking the company in the mantle of a wise and benevolent corporate institution, the public-relations people at G.E. headquarters were faced with the ugly choice of representing its role in the price-fixing affair as that of either a fool or a knave. They tended strongly toward "fool." Judge Ganey, by his statement that he assumed the conspiracies to have been not only condoned but approved by the top brass and the company as a whole, clearly chose "knave." But his analysis may or may not have been the right one, and after reading the Kefauver Subcommittee testimony I have come to the melancholy conclusion that the truth will very likely never be known. For, as the testimony shows, the clear waters of moral responsibility at G.E. became hopelessly muddied by a struggle to communicate—a struggle so confused that in some cases, it would now appear, if one of the big bosses at G.E. *had* ordered a subordinate to break the law, the message would somehow have been garbled in its reception, and if the subordinate *had* informed the boss that he was holding conspiratorial meetings with competitors, the boss might well have been under the impression that the subordinate was gossiping idly about lawn parties or pinochle sessions. Specifically, it would appear that a subordinate who received a direct oral order from his boss had to figure out whether it meant what it seemed to or the exact opposite, while the boss, in conversing with a subordinate, had to figure out whether he should take what the man told *him* at face value or should attempt to translate it out of a secret code to which he was by no means sure he had the key. That was the problem in a nutshell, and I state it here thus baldly as a suggestion for any potential beneficiary of a foundation who may be casting about for a suitable project on which to draw up a prospectus.

For the past eight years or so, G.E. has had a company rule called Directive Policy 20.5, which reads, in part, "No employee shall enter into any understanding, agreement, plan or scheme, expressed or implied, formal or informal, with any competitor, in regard to prices, terms or conditions of sale, production, distribution, territories, or customers; nor exchange or discuss with a competitor prices, terms or conditions of sale, or any other competitive information." In effect, this rule is simply an injunction to G.E.'s personnel to obey the federal antitrust laws, except that it is somewhat more concrete and comprehensive in the matter of price than they are. It is almost impossible for executives with jurisdiction over pricing policies at G.E. to be unaware of 20.5, or even hazy about it, because to make sure that new executives are acquainted with it and to refresh the memories of old ones, the company formally reissues and distributes it at intervals, and all such executives are asked to sign their names to it as an earnest that they are currently complying with it and intend to keep on doing so. The trouble—at least during the period covered by the court action, and apparently for a long time before that as well—was that some people at G.E., including some of those who regularly signed 20.5, simply did not believe that it was to be taken seriously. They assumed that 20.5 was mere window dressing: that it was on the books solely to provide legal protection for the company and for the higher-ups; that meeting illegally with competitors was recognized and accepted as standard practice within the company; and that often when a ranking executive ordered a subordinate executive to comply with 20.5, he was actually ordering him to violate it. Illogical as it might seem, this last assumption becomes comprehensible in the light of the fact that, for a time, when some executives orally conveyed, or reconveyed, the order, they were apparently in the habit of accompanying it with an unmistakable wink. In May of 1948, for example, there was a meeting of G.E. sales managers during which the custom of winking was openly discussed. Robert Paxton, an upper-level G.E. executive who later became the company's president, addressed the meeting and delivered the usual admonition about antitrust violations, whereupon William S. Ginn, then a sales executive in the transformer division, under Paxton's authority, startled him by saying, "I didn't see you wink." Paxton replied firmly, "There was no wink. We mean it, and these are the orders." Asked by Senator Kefauver how long he had been aware that orders issued at G.E. were sometimes accompanied by winks, Paxton replied that he had first observed the practice way back in 1935, when his boss had given him an instruction along with a wink or its equivalent, and that when, some time later, the significance of the gesture dawned on him, he had become so incensed that he had with difficulty restrained himself from jeopardizing his career by punching the boss in the nose. Paxton went on to say that his objections to the practice of winking had been so strong as to earn him a reputation in the company for being an antiwink man, and that he, for his part, had never winked.

Although Paxton would seem to have left little doubt as to how he intended his winkless order of 1948 to be interpreted, its meaning failed to get through to Ginn, for not long after it was issued, he went out and fixed prices to a fare-thee-well. (Obviously, it takes more than one company to make a price-fixing agreement, but all the testimony tends to indicate that it was G.E. that generally set the pattern for the rest of the industry in such matters.) Thirteen years later, Ginn —fresh from a few weeks in jail, and fresh out of a $135,000-a-year job—appeared before the Subcommittee to account for, among other things, his strange response to the winkless order. He had disregarded it, he said, because he had received a contrary order from two of his other superiors in the G.E. chain of command, Henry V. B. Erben and Francis Fairman, and in explaining why he had heeded their order rather than Paxton's he introduced the fascinating concept of degrees of communication—another theme for a foundation grantee to get his teeth into. Erben and Fairman, Ginn said, had been more articulate, persuasive, and forceful in issuing their order than Paxton had been in issuing his; Fairman, especially, Ginn stressed, had proved to be "a great communicator, a great philosopher, and, frankly, a great believer in stability of prices." Both Erben and Fairman had dismissed Paxton as naïve, Ginn testified, and, in further summary of how he had been led astray, he said that "the people who were advocating the Devil were able to sell me better than the philosophers that were selling the Lord."

It would be helpful to have at hand a report from Erben and Fairman themselves on the communication technique that enabled them to prevail over Paxton, but unfortunately neither of these philosophers could testify before the Subcommittee, because by the time of the hearings both of them were dead. Paxton, who was available, was described in Ginn's testimony as having been at all times one of the philosopher-salesmen on the side of the Lord. "I can clarify Mr. Paxton by saying Mr. Paxton came closer to being an Adam Smith advocate than any businessman I have met in America," Ginn declared. Still, in 1950, when Ginn admitted to Paxton in casual conversation that he had "compromised himself" in respect to antitrust matters, Paxton merely told him that he was a damned fool, and did not report the confession to anyone else in the company. Testifying as to why he did not, Paxton said that when the conversation occurred he was no longer Ginn's boss, and that, in the light of his personal ethics, repeating such an admission by a man not under his authority would be "gossip" and "talebearing."

Meanwhile, Ginn, no longer answerable to Paxton, was meeting with competitors at frequent intervals and moving steadily up the corporate ladder. In November, 1954, he was made general manager of the transformer division, whose headquarters were in Pittsfield, Massachusetts—a job that put him in line for a vice-presidency. At the time of Ginn's shift, Ralph J. Cordiner, who has been chairman of the board of General Electric since 1949, called him down to New York for the express purpose of enjoining him to comply strictly and undeviatingly with Directive Policy 20.5. Cordiner communicated this idea so successfully that it was clear enough to Ginn at the moment, but it remained so only as long as it took him, after leaving the chairman, to walk to Erben's office. There his comprehension of what he had just heard became clouded. Erben, who was head of G.E.'s distribution group, ranked directly below Cordiner and directly above Ginn, and, according to Ginn's testimony, no sooner were they alone in his office than he countermanded Cordiner's injunction, saying, "Now, keep on doing the way that you have been doing, but just be sensible about it and use your head on the subject." Erben's extraordinary communicative prowess again carried the day, and Ginn continued to meet with competitors. "I knew Mr. Cordiner could fire me," he told Senator Kefauver, "but also I knew I was working for Mr. Erben."

At the end of 1954, Paxton took over Erben's job and thereby became Ginn's boss again. Ginn went right on meeting with competitors, but, since he was aware that Paxton disapproved of the practice, didn't tell him about it. Moreover, he testified, within a month or two he had become convinced that he could not afford to discontinue attending the meetings under any circumstances, for in January, 1955, the entire electrical-equipment industry became embroiled in a drastic price war —known as the "white sale," because of its timing and the bargains it afforded to buyers—in which the erstwhile amiable competitors began fiercely undercutting one another. Such a manifestation of free enterprise was, of course, exactly what the intercompany conspiracies were intended to prevent, but just at that time the supply of electrical apparatus so greatly exceeded the demand that first a few of the conspirators and then more and more began breaking the agreements they themselves had made. In dealing with the situation as best he could, Ginn said, he "used the philosophies that had been taught me previously"—by which he meant that he continued to conduct price-fixing meetings, in the hope that at least *some* of the agreements made at them would be honored. As for Paxton, in Ginn's opinion that philosopher was not only ignorant of the meetings but so constant in his devotion to the concept of free and aggressive competition that he actually enjoyed the price war, disastrous though it was to everybody's profits. (In his own testimony, Paxton vigorously denied that he had enjoyed it.)

Within a year or so, the electrical-equipment industry took an upturn, and in January, 1957, Ginn, having ridden out the storm relatively well, got his vice-presidency. At the same time, he was transferred to Schenectady, to become general manager of G.E.'s turbine-generator division, and Cordiner again called him into headquarters and gave him a lecture on 20.5. Such lectures were getting to be a routine with Cordiner; every time a new employee was assigned to a strategic managerial post, or an old employee was promoted to such a post, the lucky fellow could be reasonably certain that he would be summoned to the chairman's office to hear a rendition of the austere creed. In his book *The Heart of Japan,* Alexander Campbell reports that a large Japanese electrical concern has drawn up a list of seven company commandments (for example, "Be courteous and sincere!"), and that each morning, in each of its thirty factories, the workers are required to stand at attention and recite these in unison, and then to sing the company song ("For ever-increasing production/Love your work, give your all!"). Cordiner did not require his subordinates to recite or sing 20.5—as far as is known, he never even had it set to music—but from the number of times men like Ginn had it read to them or otherwise recalled to their attention, they must have come to know it well enough to chant it, improvising a tune as they went along.

This time, Cordiner's message not only made an impression on Ginn's mind but stuck there in unadulterated form. Ginn, according to his testimony, became a reformed executive and dropped his price-fixing habits overnight. However, it appears that his sudden conversion cannot be attributed wholly to Cordiner's powers of communication, or even to the drip-drip-drip effect of repetition, for it was to a considerable extent pragmatic in character, like the conversion of Henry VIII to Protestantism. He reformed, Ginn explained to the Subcommittee, because his "air cover was gone."

"Your what was gone?" Senator Kefauver asked.

"My air cover was gone," replied Ginn. "I mean I had lost my air cover. Mr. Erben wasn't around any more, and all of my colleagues had gone, and I was now working directly for Mr. Paxton, knowing his feelings on the matter. . . . Any philosophy that I had grown up with before in the past was now out the window."

If Erben, who had not been Ginn's boss since late in 1954, had been the source of his air cover, Ginn must have been without its protection for over two years, but, presumably, in the excitement of the price war he had failed to notice its absence. However that may have been, here he now was, a man suddenly shorn not only of his air cover but of his philosophy. Swiftly filling the latter void with a whole new set of principles, he circulated copies of 20.5 among his department managers in the turbine-generator division and topped this off by energetically adopting what he called a "leprosy policy"; that is, he advised his subordinates to avoid even casual social contacts with their counterparts in competing companies, because "once the relationships are established, I have come to the conclusion after many years of hard experience that the relationships tend to spread and the hanky-panky begins to get going." But now fate played a cruel trick on Ginn, and, all unknowing, he landed in the very position that Paxton and Cordiner had been in for years—that of a philosopher vainly endeavoring to sell the Lord to a flock that declined to buy his message and was, in fact, systematically engaging in the hanky-panky its leader had warned it against. Specifically, during the whole of 1957 and 1958 and the first part of 1959 two of Ginn's subordinates were piously signing 20.5 with one hand and, with the other, briskly drawing up price-fixing agreements at a whole series of meetings—in New York; Philadelphia; Chicago; Hot Springs, Virginia; and Skytop, Pennsylvania, to name a few of their gathering places.

It appears that Ginn had not been able to impart much of his shining new philosophy to others, and that at the root of his difficulty lay that old jinx, the problem of communicating. Asked at the hearings how his subordinates could possibly have gone so far astray, he replied, "I have got to admit that I made a communication error. I didn't sell this thing to the boys well enough. . . . The price is so important in the complete running of a business that, philosophically, we have got to sell people not only just the fact that it is against the law, but . . . that it shouldn't be done for many, many reasons. But it has got to be a philosophical approach and a communication approach. . . . Even though . . . I had told my associates not to do this, some of the boys did get off the reservation. . . . I have to admit to myself here an area of a failure in communications . . . which I am perfectly willing to accept my part of the responsibility for."

In earnestly striving to analyze the cause of the failure, Ginn said, he had reached the conclusion that merely issuing directives, no matter how frequently, was not enough; what was needed was "a complete philosophy, a complete understanding, a complete breakdown of barriers between people, if we are going to get some understanding and really live and manage these companies within the philosophies that they should be managed in."

Senator Hart permitted himself to comment, "You can communicate until you are dead and gone, but if the point you are communicating about, even though it be a law of the land, strikes your audience as something that is just a folklore . . . you will never sell the package."

Ginn ruefully conceded that that was true.

The concept of degrees of communication was further developed, by implication, in the testimony of another defendant, Frank E. Stehlik, who had been general manager of the G.E. low-voltage-switchgear department from May, 1956, to February, 1960. (As all but a tiny minority of the users of electricity are contentedly unaware, switchgear serves to control and protect apparatus used in the generation, conversion, transmission, and distribution of electrical energy, and around $125 million worth of it is sold annually in the United States.) Stehlik received some of his business guidance in the conventional form of orders, oral and written, and some—perhaps just as much, to judge by his testimony—through a less intellectual, more visceral medium of communication that he called "impacts." Apparently, when something happened within the company that made an impression on him, he would consult a sort of internal metaphysical voltmeter to ascertain the force of the jolt that he had received, and, from the reading he got, would attempt to gauge the true drift of company policy. For example, he testified that during 1956, 1957, and most of 1958 he believed that G.E. was frankly and fully in favor of complying with 20.5. But then, in the autumn of 1958, George E. Burens, Stehlik's immediate superior, told him that he, Burens, had been directed by Paxton, who by then was president of G.E., to have lunch with Max Scott, president of the I-T-E Circuit Breaker Company, an important competitor in the switchgear market. Paxton said in his own testimony that while he had indeed asked Burens to have lunch with Scott, he had instructed him categorically not to talk about prices, but apparently Burens did not mention this caveat to Stehlik; in any event, the disclosure that the high command had told Burens to lunch with an archrival, Stehlik testified, "had a heavy impact on me." Asked to amplify this, he said, "There are a great many impacts that influence me in my thinking as to the true attitude of the company, and that was one of them." As the impacts, great and small, piled up, their cumulative effect finally communicated to Stehlik that he had been wrong in supposing the company had any real respect for 20.5. Accordingly, when, late in 1958, Stehlik was ordered by Burens to begin holding price meetings with the competitors, he was not in the least surprised.

Stehlik's compliance with Burens' order ultimately brought on a

in doing this, he said, because he was convinced that both in company circles and in the whole industry negotiations of this kind were "the order of the day."

By the time Vinson became his superior, in October, Smith was regularly attending price-fixing meetings, and he felt that he ought to let his new boss know what he was doing. Accordingly, he told the Subcommittee, on two or three occasions when the two men found themselves alone together in the normal course of business, he said to Vinson, "I had a meeting with the clan this morning." Counsel for the Subcommittee asked Smith whether he had ever put the matter more bluntly—whether, for example, he had ever said anything like "We're meeting with competitors to fix prices. We're going to have a little conspiracy here and I don't want it to get out." Smith replied that he had never said anything remotely like that—had done nothing more than make remarks on the order of "I had a meeting with the clan this morning." He did not elaborate on why he did not speak with greater directness, but two logical possibilities present themselves. Perhaps he hoped that he could keep Vinson informed about the situation and at the same time protect him from the risk of becoming an accomplice. Or perhaps he had no such intention, and was simply expressing himself in the oblique, colloquial way that characterized much of his speaking. (Paxton, a close friend of Smith's, had once complained to Smith that he was "given to being somewhat cryptic" in his remarks.) Anyhow, Vinson, according to his own testimony, had flatly misunderstood what Smith meant; indeed, he could not recall ever hearing Smith use the expression "meeting of the clan," although he did recall his saying things like "Well, I am going to take this new plan on transformers and show it to the boys." Vinson testified that he had thought the "boys" meant the G.E. district sales people and the company's customers, and that the "new plan" was a new marketing plan; he said that it had come as a rude shock to him to learn—a couple of years later, after the case had broken—that in speaking of the "boys" and the "new plan," Smith had been referring to competitors and a price-fixing scheme. "I think Mr. Smith is a sincere man," Vinson testified. "I am sure Mr. Smith . . . thought he was telling me that he was going to one of these meetings. This meant nothing to me."

Smith, on the other hand, was confident that his meaning had got through to Vinson. "I never got the impression that he misunderstood me," he insisted to the Subcommittee. Questioning Vinson later, Kefauver asked whether an executive in his position, with thirty-odd years' experience in the electrical industry, could possibly be so naïve as to misunderstand a subordinate on such a substantive matter as grasping who the "boys" were. "I don't think it is too naïve," replied Vinson. "We have a lot of boys. . . . I may be naïve, but I am certainly telling the truth, and in this kind of thing I am sure I am naïve."

> SENATOR KEFAUVER: Mr. Vinson, you wouldn't be a vice-president at $200,000 a year if you were naïve.
>
> MR. VINSON: I think I could well get there by being naïve in this area. It might help.

Here, in a different field altogether, the communication problem again comes to the fore. Was Vinson really saying to Kefauver what he seemed to be saying—that naïveté about antitrust violations might be a help to a man in getting and holding a $200,000-a-year job at General Electric? It seems unlikely. And yet what else could he have meant? Whatever the answer, neither the federal antitrust men nor the Senate investigators were able to prove that Smith succeeded in his attempts to communicate to Vinson the fact that he was engaging in price-fixing. And, lacking such proof, they were unable to establish what they gave every appearance of going all out to establish if they could: namely, that at least some one man at the pinnacle of G.E.'s management—some member of the sacred executive committee itself

—was implicated. Actually, when the story of the conspiracies first became known, Vinson not only concurred in a company decision to punish Smith by drastically demoting him but personally informed him of the decision—two acts that, if he had grasped Smith's meaning back in 1957, would have denoted a remarkable degree of cynicism and hypocrisy. (Smith, by the way, rather than accept the demotion, quit General Electric and, after being fined three thousand dollars and given a suspended thirty-day prison sentence by Judge Ganey, found a job elsewhere, at ten thousand dollars a year.)

This was not Vinson's only brush with the case. He was also among those named in one of the grand jury indictments that precipitated the court action, this time in connection not with his comprehension of Smith's jargon but with the conspiracy in the switchgear department. On this aspect of the case, four switchgear executives—Burens, Stehlik, Clarence E. Burke, and H. Frank Hentschel—testified before the grand jury (and later before the Subcommittee) that at some time in July, August, or September of 1958 (none of them could establish the precise date) Vinson had had lunch with them in Dining Room B of G.E.'s switchgear works in Philadelphia, and that during the meal he had instructed them to hold price meetings with competitors. As a result of this order, they said, a meeting attended by representatives of G.E., Westinghouse, the Allis-Chalmers Manufacturing Company, the Federal Pacific Electric Company, and the I-T-E Circuit Breaker Company was held at the Hotel Traymore in Atlantic City on November 9, 1958, at which sales of switchgear to federal, state, and municipal agencies were divvied up, with General Electric to get 39 percent of the business, Westinghouse 35 percent, I-T-E 11 percent, Allis-Chalmers 8 percent, and Federal Pacific Electric 7 percent. At subsequent meetings, agreement was reached on allocating sales of switchgear to private buyers as well, and an elaborate formula was worked out whereby the privilege of submitting the lowest bid to prospective customers was rotated among the conspiring companies at two-week intervals. Because of its periodic nature, this was called the phase-of-the-moon formula—a designation that in due time led to the following lyrical exchange between the Subcommittee and L. W. Long, an executive of Allis-Chalmers:

> SENATOR KEFAUVER: Who were the phasers-of-the-mooners—phase-of-the-mooners?
>
> MR. LONG: As it developed, this so-called phase-of-the-moon operation was carried out at a level below me, I think referred to as a working group. . . .
>
> MR. FERRALL [counsel for the Subcommittee]: Did they ever report to you about it?
>
> MR. LONG: Phase of the moon? No.

Vinson told the Justice Department prosecutors, and repeated to the Subcommittee, that he had not known about the Traymore meeting, the phase-of-the-mooners, or the existence of the conspiracy itself until the case broke; as for the lunch in Dining Room B, he insisted that it had never taken place. On this point, Burens, Stehlik, Burke, and Hentschel submitted to lie-detector tests, administered by the F.B.I., and passed them. Vinson refused to take a lie-detector test, at first explaining that he was acting on advice of counsel and against his personal inclination, and later, after hearing how the four other men had fared, arguing that if the machine had not pronounced them liars, it couldn't be any good. It was established that on only eight business days during July, August, and September had Burens, Burke, Stehlik, and Hentschel all been together in the Philadelphia plant at the lunch hour, and Vinson produced some of his expense accounts, which, he pointed out to the Justice Department, showed that he had been elsewhere on each of those days. Confronted with this evidence, the Justice Department dropped its case against Vinson, and he has stayed on as a vice-president of General Electric. Nothing that the Subcommittee elicited from him cast any substantive doubt on the defense that had impressed the government prosecutors.

Thus, the uppermost echelon at G.E. came through unscathed; the record showed that participation in the conspiracy went fairly far down in the organization but not all the way to the top. Gezon, everybody agreed, had followed orders from Stehlik, and Stehlik had followed orders from Burens, but that was the end of the trail, because although Burens said he had followed orders from Vinson, Vinson denied it and made the denial stick. The government, at the end of its investigation, stated in court that it could not prove, and did not claim, that either Chairman Cordiner or President Paxton had authorized, or even known about, the conspiracies, and thereby officially ruled out the possibility that they had resorted to at least a figurative wink. Later, Paxton and Cordiner showed up in Washington to testify before the Subcommittee, and its interrogators were similarly unable to establish that they had ever indulged in any variety of winking.

After being described by Ginn as General Electric's stubbornest and most dedicated advocate of free competition, Paxton explained to the Subcommittee that his thinking on the subject had been influenced not directly by Adam Smith but, rather, by way of a former G.E. boss he had worked under—the late Gerard Swope. Swope, Paxton testified, had always believed firmly that the ultimate goal of business was to produce more goods for more people at lower cost. "I bought that then, I buy it now," said Paxton. "I think it is the most marvelous statement of economic philosophy that any industrialist has ever expressed." In the course of his testimony, Paxton had an explanation, philosophical or otherwise, of each of the several situations related to price-fixing in which his name had earlier been mentioned. For instance, it had been brought out that in 1956 or 1957 a young man named Jerry Page, a minor employee in G.E.'s switchgear division, had written directly to Cordiner alleging that the switchgear divisions of G.E. and of several competitor companies were involved in a conspiracy in which information about prices was exchanged by means of a secret code based on different colors of letter paper. Cordiner had turned the matter over to Paxton with orders that he get to the bottom of it, and Paxton had thereupon conducted an investigation that led him to conclude that the color-code conspiracy was "wholly a hallucination on the part of this boy." In arriving at that conclusion, Paxton had apparently been right, although it later came out that there had been a conspiracy in the switchgear division during 1956 and 1957; this, however, was a rather conventional one, based simply on price-fixing meetings, rather than on anything so gaudy as a color code. Page could not be called to testify because of ill health.

Paxton conceded that there had been some occasions when he "must have been pretty damn dumb." (Dumb or not, for his services as the company's president he was, of course, remunerated on a considerably grander scale than Vinson—receiving a basic annual salary of $125,-000, plus annual incentive compensation of about $175,000, plus stock options designed to enable him to collect much more, at the comparatively low tax rate on capital gains, if General Electric's stock should go up.) As for Paxton's attitude toward company communications, he emerges as a pessimist on this score. Upon being asked at the hearings to comment on the Smith-Vinson conversations of 1957, he said that, knowing Smith, he just could not "cast the man in the role of a liar," and went on:

> When I was younger, I used to play a good deal of bridge. We played about fifty rubbers of bridge, four of us, every winter, and I think we probably played some rather good bridge. If you gentlemen are bridge players, you know that there is a code of signals

> that is exchanged between partners as the game progresses. It is a stylized form of playing. . . . Now, as I think about this—and I was particularly impressed when I read Smith's testimony when he talked about a "meeting of the clan" or "meeting of the boys"—I begin to think that there must have been a stylized method of communication between these people who were dealing with competition. Now, Smith could say, "I told Vinson what I was doing," and Vinson wouldn't have the foggiest idea what was being told to him, and both men could testify under oath, one saying yes and the other man saying no, and both be telling the truth. . . . [They] wouldn't be on the same wavelength. [They] wouldn't have the same meanings. I think, I believe now that these men did think that they were telling the truth, but they weren't communicating between each other with understanding.

Here, certainly, is the gloomiest possible analysis of the communications problem.

Chairman Cordiner's status, it appears from his testimony, was approximately that of the Boston Cabots in the celebrated jingle. His services to the company, for which he was recompensed in truly handsome style (with, for 1960, a salary of just over $280,000, plus contingent deferred income of about $120,000, plus stock options potentially worth hundreds of thousands more), were indubitably many and valuable, but they were performed on such an exalted level that, at least in antitrust matters, he does not seem to have been able to have any earthly communication at all. When he emphatically told the Subcommittee that at no time had he had so much as an inkling of the network of conspiracies, it could be deduced that his was a case not of faulty communication but of no communication. He did not speak to the Subcommittee of philosophy or philosophers, as Ginn and Paxton had done, but from his past record of ordering reissues of 20.5 and of peppering his speeches and public statements with praise of free enterprise, it seems clear that he was *un philosophe sans le savoir*—and one on the side of selling the Lord, since no evidence was adduced to suggest that he was given to winking in any form. Kefauver ran through a long list of antitrust violations of which General Electric had been accused over the past half-century, asking Cordiner, who joined the company in 1922, how much he knew about each of them; usually, he replied that he had known about them only after the fact. In commenting on Ginn's testimony that Erben had countermanded Cordiner's direct order in 1954, Cordiner said that he had read it with "great alarm" and "great wonderment," since Erben had always indicated to him "an intense competitive spirit," rather than any disposition to be friendly with rival companies.

Throughout his testimony, Cordiner used the curious expression "be responsive to." If, for instance, Kefauver inadvertently asked the same question twice, Cordiner would say, "I was responsive to that a moment ago," or if Kefauver interrupted him, as he often did, Cordiner would ask politely, "May I be responsive?" This, too, offers a small lead for a foundation grantee, who might want to look into the distinction between being responsive (a passive state) and answering (an act), and their relative effectiveness in the process of communication.

Summing up his position on the case as a whole, in reply to a question of Kefauver's about whether he thought that G.E. had incurred "corporate disgrace," Cordiner said, "No, I am not going to be responsive and say that General Electric had corporate disgrace. I am going to say that we are deeply grieved and concerned. . . . I am not proud of it."

Chairman Cordiner, then, had been able to fairly deafen his subordinate officers with lectures on compliance with the rules of the company and the laws of the country, but he had not been able to get all those officers to comply with either, and President Paxton could muse thoughtfully on how it was that two of his subordinates who had given radically different accounts of a conversation between them could be not liars but merely poor communicators. Philosophy seems to have reached a high point at G.E., and communication a low one. If executives could just learn to understand one another, most of the witnesses said or implied, the problem of antitrust violations would be solved. But perhaps the problem is cultural as well as technical, and has something to do with a loss of personal identity that comes from working in a huge organization. The cartoonist Jules Feiffer, contemplating the communication problem in a nonindustrial context, has said, "Actually, the breakdown is between the person and himself. If you're not able to communicate successfully between yourself and yourself, how are you supposed to make it with the strangers outside?" Suppose, purely as a hypothesis, that the owner of a company who orders his subordinates to obey the antitrust laws has such poor communication with himself that he does not really know whether he wants the order to be complied with or not. If his order is disobeyed, the resulting price-fixing may benefit his company's coffers; if it is obeyed, then he has done the right thing. In the first instance, he is not personally implicated in any wrongdoing, while in the second he is positively involved in *right*doing. What, after all, can he lose? It is perhaps reasonable to suppose that such an executive might communicate his uncertainty more forcefully than his order. Possibly yet another foundation grantee should have a look at the reverse of communication failure, where he might discover that messages the sender does not even realize he is sending sometimes turn out to have got across only too effectively.

Meanwhile, in the first year after the Subcommittee concluded its investigation, the defendant companies were by no means allowed to forget their transgressions. The law permits customers who can prove that they have paid artificially high prices as a result of anti-trust violations to sue for damages—in most cases, triple damages—and suits running into many millions of dollars soon began piling up. (By January, 1962, they had piled up so high that Chief Justice Warren set up a special panel of federal judges to plan how they should all be handled.) Needless to say, Cordiner was not allowed to forget about the matter, either; indeed, it would be surprising if he was allowed a chance to think about much else, for, in addition to the suits, he had to contend with active efforts by a minority group of stockholders to unseat him. Paxton retired as president in April, 1961, because of ill health dating back at least to the previous January, when he underwent a major operation. As for the executives who pleaded guilty and were fined or imprisoned, most of those who had been employed by companies other than G.E. remained with them, either in their old jobs or in similar ones. Of those who had been employed by G.E., none remained there. Some retired permanently from business, others settled for comparatively small jobs, and a few landed big ones—most spectacularly Ginn, who in June, 1961, became president of Baldwin-Lima-Hamilton, manufacturers of heavy machinery. And as for the future of price-fixing in the electrical industry, it seems safe to say that what with the Justice Department, Judge Ganey, Senator Kefauver, and the triple-damage suits, the impact on the philosophers who guide corporate policy has been such that they, and even their subordinates, are likely to try to hew scrupulously to the line for quite some time. Quite a different question, however, is whether they have made any headway in their ability to communicate.

6 / Thaw on Threadneedle Street

THE NINETEENTH-CENTURY British economist Walter Bagehot called the City—that is, the old City of London, which is the British equivalent of Wall Street—"by far the greatest combination of economical power and economical delicacy that the world has ever seen." What Bagehot meant by "delicacy" undoubtedly embraced, among other things, a reserve sometimes bordering on iciness—particularly in dealings with strangers—that is said to characterize London's financiers in the twentieth century no less than it did in the nineteenth. Even the loyally British publication the *Economist*, of which I have been a sporadic reader for several years, speaks a bit guardedly of the City's "veil of privacy." Such a reputation for cool imperviousness naturally tends to affect an inquisitive transatlantic visitor—and especially one like me, who has spent quite a lot of time snooping around the platforms and board rooms of Wall Street—very much as Mount Everest affected Mallory. So when I found myself on the loose in London for a few days in the autumn of 1960, I resolved to have a go at cracking the City's reticence; before I was through, I ran into plenty of delicacy, no iciness to speak of, and intimations, at least, of power.

It might be thought—anyway, it was by me—that an American hoping to slip behind the City's veil would need some language training, the local dialect being what it is. I considered myself fortunate in this respect, for my years of puzzling over the *Economist* had amounted to a Berlitz course. As things turned out, though, I was given no opportunity to show that I knew how to translate into British such American terms as mutual funds (unit trusts), installment debt (hire-purchase debt), and investment and commercial banking (merchant banking). Nevertheless, my training served a purpose, for it enabled me to tackle the City with the comforting knowledge that the same, or similar, institutions flourish on both sides of the Atlantic, however different the local folkways may be. A buck is a buck and a quid is a quid; introduce a factor of about 2.81, and bucks turn into quids or quids into bucks. Another confidence-builder was the fact that at the time I was in London, the stock market there was straining toward an all-time high. In Wall Street, I have always found, there is nothing like a good market to thaw out economical delicacy, just as there is nothing like a bad market to freeze it up.

Indeed, when I emerged from the Underground station outside the Bank of England one drizzly morning, I got the impression that the City was in a friendly and expansive mood. Probably this feeling came in considerable part from the presence everywhere of flowers, which are so bleakly absent from Wall Street. As I wandered around the central streets of the City, I discovered that almost every one of the buildings, however massive and soot-blackened, had flowerboxes on its window ledges or out on the sidewalk—mainly at that time containing late-blooming varieties, like chrysanthemums. As for the people on the streets, they looked cheerful enough, in a self-possessed way. This was most notably true of certain gentlemen wearing black suits and top hats; these men, I knew, were bill brokers—members of a small and ineffably respectable fraternity whose function is to keep capital flowing around the City by borrowing from firms that temporarily have too much money on hand and lending to firms that haven't enough. Wall Street has no bill brokers, and it could use some, if only to give the place a little tone. Out of curiosity, I followed a bill broker at a decent distance as he proceeded with a purposeful but unhurried stride along Poultry, past Old Jewry, and on to the corner of Queen Street, where he met another of his kind. The two of them nodded, their hats giving the gesture a certain exaggerated quality, and after conversing for a moment on the sidewalk they both entered a building labeled Ghana Commercial Bank. Capital, I took it, would soon be flowing.

Circling back, I began to notice right and left the City's similarities to Wall Street—or, rather, to avoid provincial ethnocentrism, Wall Street's similarities to the City. There were the same long black cars disgorging men of substance in front of their offices. There were the same little alleys largely monopolized by pedestrians, the same new glass-walled buildings interspersed here and there among the predominant heavy old stone ones, the same nondescript side streets lined with loft buildings whose ground floors were occupied by shops selling luggage, office equipment, and stamp collectors' items. (A natural law of money: The presence of great quantities of it tends to impose a certain pattern on the surroundings, the way a magnet imposes a pattern on iron filings.) Furthermore, the old (and now no longer functioning) Royal Exchange, a Corinthian temple standing at the key intersection of the City, where Threadneedle Street and Cornhill meet, suggested our Subtreasury Building—the Corinthian temple at the intersection of Wall and Nassau. Venturing to enter the Royal Exchange, I found that it was now largely given over to an exhibition of City antiquities, including some coins from the time of Julius Caesar, and even earlier. (Another natural law: Money, once established in a certain place, tends to stay there.) Some of the old coins had been unearthed recently, and a sign urged anyone who found such coins, in the course of scrabbling in City soil, to turn them in. With British thoroughness, the sign invoked both authority and reason by pointing out that, in the first place, the law required that old coins be turned in, and that, in the second, it was to the finders' own advantage to turn them in, since they were worth more as museum pieces than as precious metal.

Glancing back as I left the Royal Exchange, I observed on its architrave the quotation, "The Earth is the Lord's and the fulness thereof." It was hard—impossible, rather—to resist the cynical thought that insofar as gold bullion may be said to represent the earth's fullness, quite a bit of it just then was the Bank of England's (the Bank is the fiscal agent for the British government), and was at that very moment reposing in the depths of that institution, right across Threadneedle Street from where I was standing. There were some benches on the sidewalk opposite the Bank, and I sat there for a while looking at the building. It reminded me of a mammoth mausoleum, its high ground floor unrelieved by a single window, its doors like those usually found on vaults. Its custodians, however, had not felt impelled to adorn it with flowers. I was thinking that, to judge by the front it presented, the Bank carried reticence well beyond the point of economical delicacy when I saw with a sense of relief—almost of shock—a couple of blithe young secretaries sashay in through that seemingly impenetrable entrance. But they had certain advantages I lacked, and I recalled the experience of an Englishman I had read about who approached the Bank for reasons similar to mine and, on being ushered into the presence of one of its officers, asked what his duties were. "To protect Bank officials from the likes of you, if you don't mind my saying so," the officer replied. I decided to pass up the Bank—at least for that day.

Instead, I started with the London Stock Exchange, knowing that, like all stock exchanges in this age of distributed wealth, it is democratically inclined, and has gone so far as to emulate the New York Stock Exchange by installing a visitors' gallery. I reached the gallery by climbing one flight from an entrance at 8 Throgmorton Street, right around the corner from the Bank, and then walking through a couple of reception rooms decorated with modern furniture, pamphlets, and pretty girl guides. It was all just as it is in New York, except for one thing: in London you can scarcely look at any of the rooms' furnishings—a curtain, say, or a section of wallpaper—without finding a reproduction of the London Stock Exchange coat of arms and motto, *"Dictum Meum Pactum."* It isn't long before one of the pretty girls helpfully informs you that this means "My word is my bond." The gallery is very much like the New York gallery, except that in London the visitor is separated from the floor by a pane of glass. As for the floor itself, though it is less capacious than New York's, the brokers and traders on it are just as fond of littering it with small pieces of paper and almost as fond of engaging in fake fist fights and other forms of horseplay. The London floor, however, is enviably brightened by the presence around the perimeter of numerous men wearing red-and-navy-blue uniforms and top hats with gold piping, who at intervals utter weird, singsong cries, audible even through the pane of glass and reminiscent of the cries of actors in Japanese *no* drama. Moreover, the London floor has a good many benches. In London, a Stock Exchange membership is called a membership, and it entitles the holder to take a seat; in New York, a Stock Exchange membership is called a seat, and, as I need not remind the toilers at 11 Wall, there is practically no place to sit.

While I watched it all, along with a couple of dozen other visitors, one of the girls offered explanations. She told us that the garishly dressed men were attendants, that their unearthly cries summoned brokers to the telephone, and that they are called "waiters" out of deference to the coffeehouse origins of the London Stock Exchange. She also explained that the passage of time toward the end of each trading day is marked by a series of three rattles. The first, at two-fifteen, serves warning that no deals made thereafter will be settled until the following morning; the second informs the members that it is three-fifteen, and time for smokers to light up, if they wish; and the third, fifteen minutes later, announces the closing. Lastly, our guide called our attention to twelve pillars on the floor, around which most of the trading was being done, and said they were known as pitches. Having finished her spiel, she wanted to know if there were any questions.

I had one all ready. "Why are the pillars called pitches?" I asked.

"Why do you call them pillars?" she shot back, giving me a melting smile.

Since I couldn't think of anything to say to that, I assumed that the Old World had stolen a march on the New, until I found out later that she wasn't quite accurate. The pillars themselves aren't called pitches; the trading places at their bases are, because it is there that a dealer—or, to translate the word into British, a "jobber"—makes his pitch.

After the questions and answers, our girl guide led us into a small theater, where we saw a twenty-three-minute film entitled *My Word Is My Bond*. In brilliant color, it outlined the history of the London Stock Exchange and went on to present a little sketch of an apple-cheeked British couple visiting a broker to make their first investment; supposedly showing how the Exchange works today, it was liberally laced with ringing affirmations driven home by kettledrums—affirmations like (and I quote from memory, since it was too dark to write in the theater) "The City and the Stock Exchange are synonymous with honesty, fair dealing, and integrity." (Bong! Bong!) The New York Stock Exchange has a film, too; it is twenty-seven minutes long, and before getting down, briefly, to the brass tacks of buying stock it presents a hazy pageant of American science and industry, accompanied by ringing affirmations like "Investors have helped create jobs for millions." (No kettledrums.) In cinematic art, I decided, it was a standoff between the two great institutions.

At the end of the film, I asked the guide what the chances were for me to round out my visit by spending five minutes or so with an official of the Exchange. She picked up a phone, and reported a moment later that Mr. Simon Preston, of the public-relations department, would see me right away in his office, on the first floor at 23 Throgmorton Street. I concealed my surprise at learning that the Exchange *had* a public-relations department, and simply thanked the girl and made my way to 23 Throgmorton, where I rose breathtakingly to the first floor (it's one flight up in England, of course) in a contraption that seemed the perfect embodiment of the Exchange's odd mixture of old and new—a nineteenth-century open-grillwork elevator that had been converted to self-service. Mr. Preston, a smiling, fair-haired, youngish man, debonair of manner and public-school of speech, told me apologetically that he might be interrupted while we were talking; one of the companies listed on the Exchange was suspected of some fishy dealings, the Exchange had just turned over certain information to the police, and, as a result of these developments, he was in a bash. He didn't look it, though; he looked as calm as Nelson at Trafalgar. "Been to the gallery, have you?" he said. "You saw *My Word Is My Bond,* I suppose, and the *'Dictum Meum Pactum'* wallpaper? They adopted that motto when the Exchange was organized, in 1773. Possibly it annoys you slightly? We emphasize it because that is considered one of the nicest aspects of this business—nothing written down, all deals made orally and later adhered to. Same thing on your Exchange, to be sure, but since we have the motto, we like to use it. Admittedly, we rather cherish our traditions. For example, dark suits to be worn on the floor at all times, and black hats, if any. Members occasionally show up wearing funny hats. They are immediately seized upon and torn to pieces by other members. I mean the hats. One old boy wears a straw boater once a year, on his birthday, for a lark. It gets destroyed regularly."

A moment later, a pleasant-looking man entered the room. Mr. Preston introduced him to me as Lord Ritchie of Dundee, chairman of the Stock Exchange Council, and the two men then engaged in a short conversation about the bash. I promised I wouldn't reproduce it, and I won't. *Dictum meum pactum.* When Lord Ritchie had left, Mr. Preston fell into a statistical mood and gave me some figures to account for the greatness of the London Stock Exchange. It lists about 9,500 securities, while 1,500 are listed by the New York Stock Exchange. It has about 3,500 members to New York's 1,400. Its members include more than a dozen peers; New York gets whitewashed there. Becoming a member—and I'll drop the comparisons at this point—entails, among other things, buying a nomination from a retired member or the estate of a deceased one; the price of a nomination is regulated by supply and demand, and fluctuates wildly, depending on how appetizing a membership looks at any given time and on how many members have recently retired or died. A nomination cost sixteen hundred pounds in the autumn of 1960, but a few years ago one went for three pounds. As I gulped at this vision of a lost opportunity, Mr. Preston was interrupted by the telephone, and while he was talking he tossed me a copy of the *Stock Exchange Journal,* from which I learned that an Exchange member named W. G. Barron was chairman of the Committee on Damaged Bonds and Irregular American Certificates. I thought of asking Mr. Preston what that committee was up to, but by the time he hung up, I had decided that the question might smack of economical indelicacy. Instead, I asked him how long the London Stock Exchange had been deigning to bother about public relations. "The visitors' gallery was opened in 1953, the guides were installed in it in 1958, and the film was first shown in 1959," he replied. "Our department didn't come into being as such until the beginning of this year, although the Exchange had been making some sort of stab at public relations ever since the end of the war. Not much was accomplished in that direction, I'm afraid, during the six years of Labour Party rule. The lean years, you know." Mr. Preston smiled a confiding smile, called a secretary, and asked her to bring two cups of tea. "Now, however," he went on, "we like to think we're setting the pace for our neighbors in the City, some of whom tend to be a bit backward in this respect."

During the next couple of days, after making some preparatory telephone calls, I went on a whirlwind tour of the City, visiting N. M. Rothschild & Sons, the celebrated merchant-banking firm; Lloyd's, the —well, Lloyd's; Hoare & Company, which has the distinction of being the last surviving private-banking firm in London; and, finally, the Bank of England itself. Again and again, evidence was presented to me that economical delicacy is not necessarily incompatible with hospitality—at least, as long as the guest does not insist on talking specifically about matters economical. Perhaps one explanation of the City's easy self-assurance lies in the fact that it *is* a city, and no mean one; in contrast to Wall Street, London's financial district gets its nickname from something bigger than it is, rather than from something smaller. The City of London is an autonomous county within Greater London, consisting of 677 acres along the north bank of the Thames, and bounded by Temple Bar on the west, Aldgate on the east, and London Wall on the north. For centuries, it was the whole of London, and now, even though it is only a tiny section of the metropolis, it stubbornly retains its medieval form of government—a Lord Mayor (or, rather, the ceremonial official still known as *the* Lord Mayor of London), 25 aldermen, 206 common councilmen, and a body of liverymen, who, as representatives of the City's trade guilds, are principally charged with the duty of nominating candidates for Lord Mayor. (The guilds haven't concerned themselves with trade for centuries, but they still earn impressive incomes from property and investments, and many of them have splendid headquarters and well-filled treasuries; as Paul Ferris, an Englishman who wrote a book on the City, put it, "Most of their money is spent on schools, charities, and good food and drink.") Again in contrast to Wall Street, the vote in the City is extended to owners and renters of property as well as to its few residents, and this means that its government is in the hands of the financiers who work there, even though nearly all of them live somewhere else. Just as a good part of London, run by the London County Council, is firmly Labour, so the City is firmly Tory, as what banker or broker wouldn't be who hopes for a chance to serve a year's term as Lord Mayor of London?

At Rothschild's, which occupies a stately old mansion off St. Swithins' Lane, I was led through countless paneled and portrait-hung rooms by the firm's secretary, a kindly gentleman who asked me to cloak him in anonymity. In one of the rooms, the secretary presented a young man, who had the look of knowing what he was about, as Mr. Evelyn. I shook hands with Mr. Evelyn, and not until somewhat later, when I became more accustomed to the secretary's idiom, did I realize that the man I'd met was Mr. Evelyn de *Rothschild*. After remarking that the firm, which was founded in 1804, had recently elected its first non-

Rothschild partner ever, the secretary showed me the gold-fixing room, where, every morning, seated around an oval table and under the eyes of long-vanished European royalty looking down from the portraits on the walls, the City's four or five leading gold brokers meet to fix the day's gold price in London. Each broker has a miniature Union Jack mounted on a stand in front of him, and when, in the course of the dickering, he becomes satisfied with the price, he knocks his flag down. Nobody at Rothschild's is quite sure how the flag tradition started. All the flags are usually down within five minutes, the secretary said, but during the fevers of gold speculation that occur periodically, it sometimes takes as long as twenty or twenty-five minutes. And why is the price of gold fixed at Rothschild's? Perfectly simple, said the secretary; in the nineteenth century, between financing Wellington at Waterloo, helping to finance Britain's purchase of the Suez Canal, and putting up the cash for a few other little ventures, Rothschild's became bullion brokers for the Bank of England, and that was that.

Lloyd's, as I suppose everybody knows, is not an insurance company in the American sense but a society of individual insurers prepared to cover their losses by putting up their combined private fortunes. When I went to its headquarters on Lime Street, a fatherly sort of man named E. G. Chapman, who described himself as a clerk to the committee, led the way through a room—considerably larger and lighter than that of the London Stock Exchange—in which some men were walking around and talking to other men who were seated. Mr. Chapman explained that the rampant ones were brokers placing insurance risks and the couchant ones were underwriters assuming them. The room, he said, was called The Room. Until about five years ago, when Lloyd's moved to its present quarters from its old home on the other side of Lime Street, the brokers walked and the underwriters sat in what was really two rooms but was called The Room anyhow. On a cabinet near the center of the present Room lay a big volume full of reports on ships sunk or damaged, and Mr. Chapman advised me that entries in it are always made with a quill—not for the sake of tradition, he added firmly, but because a quill writes better on the parchment-like paper deemed appropriate for such records. He also pointed out a board suspended from one of the walls, where the names of prospective members are posted for a while prior to their admission—"like chaps being put up for a club," he remarked, leaning toward me confidentially as he spoke.

Mr. Chapman then escorted me to a large office a couple of stories above The Room, where I met Patrick Ward Milligan, deputy chairman of Lloyd's. "One decides which risks to assume on various bases," said Mr. Milligan genially, in answer to a question of mine. "First of all, experience. One has done an apprenticeship of perhaps ten years before becoming a member of Lloyd's. Then, too, perhaps the broker may be a pal of yours." The deputy chairman indicated, with a fractional grin, that he was being facetious, and went on, "Beyond that, there is your liver, the state of the weather, and so forth. Setting the premium in cases where there's no precedent is sometimes simply a matter of looking at a bare wall. The odd underwritings—insurance against holes-in-one at golf, against the capture of the Loch Ness monster, against the birth of twins, against damage to actresses' legs—are *not* an important part of our business, though I must say they are spoken of a great deal. We are rather placid here. We do not get ulcers from contemplating our liabilities. After a big storm that has cost a pretty penny in marine underwritings, you don't find everyone in The Room looking at the Loss Book. You find the crowd at the newsboard reading the test-match results."

"The deputy chairman is excessively modest," Mr. Chapman informed me as he escorted me to the front door. "It takes know-how and flair to write insurance, that's what it takes."

I had a particular reason for wanting to go to Hoare & Company.

I'd heard that among the items in a small museum of banking memorabilia that the firm has on the premises was one of the first checks, or cheques, ever written, and I was eager to see it. Accordingly, one of my telephone calls had been to the curator of this collection, making an appointment. The company's offices are in a fine old town house on Fleet Street—not as large as Rothschild's but impressive enough. An attendant led me through the ground-floor banking section, which had a sort of gaslit look, and up a long flight of stairs; on the way, he told me that one partner of the firm always lives in the building, so that clients suddenly in need of a bank in the middle of the night can get attention at once. The collection occupied a front room ornamented with a crystal chandelier, a marble mantel, and two eighteenth-century oil paintings, and there I was turned over to the curator—a peppy white-haired man, wearing a monocle and the air of a mischievous scholar, named R. McD. Winder.

"Ah, yes, the check," Mr. Winder said, going straight to the mantel, where a yellowed scrap of paper was preserved under glass.

I followed, and read:

JULY 11, 1676

MR. HOARE,

Pray pay to the bearer hereof Mr. Witt Morgan fifty-four pounds ten shillings and ten pence and take his receipt for the same.

Your loving friend,
WILL HALE

54/10/10
for Mr. Richard Hoare
at the Golden bottle in Cheapside

"We can't say that it was the first British check—only one of the first," Mr. Winder said. "Incidentally, the Golden Bottle wasn't a pub, as you might expect. It was the Hoares' place of business. They were goldsmiths, with a sideline in banking."

I asked who Will Hale was.

"Why, a Hoare client," said Mr. Winder, plainly implying that any further identification would be superfluous.

He led me to a couple of large glass cases near the windows, and pointed out various documents there enshrined. "Over here," he said, "is a record of a fund to support the suffering clergy in America during your Revolution. Hoare & Company banked the fund. And, here, a judgment of one pound against Samuel Pepys, which I do not believe you will find mentioned in his diary." Mr. Winder chuckled, and his monocle fell out. Deftly replacing it, he continued, "Here we have a copy of a letter sent by our firm to the governor of the Bank of England on the occasion of their two-hundred-and-fiftieth anniversary, in July, 1944. We're considerably older than the Bank, of course. They opened in 1694, whereas Hoare & Company was founded sometime before 1673—it has never been ascertained just when—and has been on the present site since 1689." I read the 1944 letter to the bank, and could not detect in it the slightest note of patronage toward a junior institution. A forbearing house, old Hoare & Company.

On the way out, Mr. Winder guided me into the partners' dining room for a glimpse of the inevitable collection of family portraits, calling special attention to an old fellow who, he said, had been known as Good Henry Hoare. Good Henry looked rather self-satisfied, and no wonder. I inquired whether there had ever been a Bad Henry. "No, but there was a Naughty Richard," said Mr. Winder. "Happily, he had nothing at all to do with the bank."

Mr. Winder had reminded me of the Bank of England. Screwing up my courage, I now marched on it. Well, the Old Lady of Threadneedle Street could hardly have been more gracious. An employee at the main entrance inclined his top hat solicitously while he listened to my mumbled account of myself; another accompanied me across a vast expanse of marble floor to an armored lift; a third took me up an indeterminate number of stories and showed me into a little room, where I was left alone to contemplate leather furniture and old prints for a not excessive interval; and a fourth, a young lady, escorted me into the presence of a Bank officer, who did not tell me what his duties were. (I took pains not to ask.) The officer—I'll call him Harris, for he, too, asked me to suppress his identity—and I had half an hour of amiable talk, none of it about the bank rate and most of it about the Bank of England's Guard. Mr. Harris said that the Guard, consisting of an officer, a sergeant, two corporals, twelve guardsmen, and a drummer or piper, arrived at the Bank every day at the end of business hours and remained until morning, as it had been doing regularly ever since the Bank was threatened by the Gordon Riots of 1780. A while back, the War Office, noting that the rioting seemed to have subsided, suggested discontinuing the Guard, on the ground that it was costly and caused traffic jams while en route to its post. The Bank expressed horror at the mere thought of such a thing, and the War Office discreetly backed down.

"They generally arrive a bit after six o'clock," Mr. Harris said. "They're apt to come by truck if it's wet, but today's drizzle seems to be over, and they should be marching. It's not quite six. If you go right down, you should catch them all right."

That seemed to me an excellent idea, and after bidding Mr. Harris good-bye I went in reverse through the Bank's minuet of entrance. There was one hitch, though; neither I nor anyone else could remember at what stage somebody had taken my raincoat. This occasioned a good deal of whispering and scurrying around among Bank people, as, I suppose, the specter loomed of the Bank's being found guilty of having improperly appropriated an American raincoat. It finally turned up, and, to everyone's relief, the Old Lady and I parted all even.

I sat down on one of the benches across Threadneedle Street, and at five minutes past six the Guard arrived, marching smartly up in three admirably regular columns, all red-coated and busby-topped. True to Harris' count, there were seventeen men in all, but if one was a drummer or piper, he wasn't drumming or piping. The Guard came to a stamping halt in front of the Bank, and at the officer's command the guardsmen filed in through the entrance. I noticed that nearly all the civilian Britons who happened to be passing on their way home from work stopped to watch. They must see this delightful folderol almost every day, I reflected, and yet they did not seem to be at all bored by it; most of them were grinning the same sort of half-moved, half-sheepish grin that I was.

About the Author

John Brooks was born in New York City on December 5, 1920. Until he was four he lived in Douglaston, Long Island; then his family moved to Trenton, New Jersey, where he lived until after the war. He now resides in Greenwich Village, New York, with his wife and two children.

Mr. Brooks was educated at the Kent School in Kent, Connecticut, and at Princeton University. At Princeton, he edited the *Daily Princetonian* and majored in English literature. After his graduation, in 1942, Mr. Brooks joined the army the following month. He became a communications and radar man in the Air Force. At the time of D-Day he was at Normandy beach as an air liaison man aboard the First Army headquarters ship.

After the war, Mr. Brooks joined the staff of *Time* magazine, where he was one of its contributing editors for two years. He has written book reviews for the *New York Times,* the New York *Herald Tribune,* and *Harper's Magazine,* and has had pieces published in national periodicals, including *The New Yorker,* to which he has been a regular contributor since 1949.

His first novel, *The Big Wheel,* was completed under a grant from the Eugene Saxton Memorial Trust and was published by Harper & Brothers in 1949. It was followed by *A Pride of Lions* (1954), *The Man Who Broke Things* (1958), and a book of nonfiction, *The Seven Fat Years* (1958).

Format by Sidney Feinberg
Set in Times Roman
Composed, printed and bound by American Book-Stratford Press, Inc.
HARPER & ROW, PUBLISHERS, INCORPORATED